Routledge Revivals

India's Balance of Indebtedness

Originally published in 1937, this study was modelled on Jacob Viner's famous work on Canada and when it was published it was an important addition to the growing literature in Applied Economics. The period selected was a time of increased foreign borrowings by India and expanding foreign demand for her products. It was also the period when the Gold Exchange Standard was being introduced into the country. The author therefore had the opportunity to find out not only whether the theory of international adjustment was borne out by India's experience but also showed to what extent, if any, the process of adjustment was affected by the peculiar currency organization. The book discusses the interrelations of foreign borrowings, the barter terms of trade and the price-level of India and throws important light on the currency controversies both old and new. The book will be of interest to students of India' economic and monetary history.

India's Balance of Indebtedness

1898–1913

Y.S. Pandit

Routledge
Taylor & Francis Group
ROUTLEDGE REVIVALS

First published in 1937 by George Allen & Unwin Ltd.

This edition first published in 2025 by Routledge
4 Park Square, Milton Park, Abingdon, Oxon, OX14 4RN
and by Routledge
605 Third Avenue, New York, NY 10158.

Routledge is an imprint of the Taylor & Francis Group, an informa business

ISBN 13: 978-1-041-07990-3 (hbk)
ISBN 13: 978-1-003-64321-0 (ebk)
ISBN 13: 978-1-041-07997-2 (pbk)
Book DOI 10.4324/9781003643210

INDIA'S BALANCE OF INDEBTEDNESS

1898-1913

by

Y. S. PANDIT, M.A.

With a Foreword by

SIR JEHANGIR COYAJEE

LONDON

GEORGE ALLEN & UNWIN LTD

MUSEUM STREET

FIRST PUBLISHED IN 1937

PRINTED IN GREAT BRITAIN BY
UNWIN BROTHERS LTD., WOKING

TO

MY MOTHER

PREFACE

This inductive study of India's balance of indebtedness during 1898 to 1913 was undertaken at the suggestion of Professor D. Ghosh of the University School of Economics and Sociology, Bombay. The work has been carried out entirely on the lines of Professor Jacob Viner's study of Canada. There were a great many difficulties in applying Viner's methods to Indian conditions, but I faced them with confidence with the help of Professor Ghosh, to whom I am greatly indebted for constant advice and criticism in completing this study.

My debt to Professor Jacob Viner, though indirect, is also equally great. The influence of his monumental work can be seen throughout the present study.

I am specially indebted to Sir Jehangir C. Coyajee who, in spite of his preoccupations, kindly consented to write a Foreword to this book.

I also acknowledge my indebtedness to the University of Bombay for the substantial financial help it has granted towards the cost of the publication of this book.

Y. S. PANDIT

BOMBAY

October 1936

FOREWORD

In 1924 Jacob Viner—an eminent American Professor—published his famous and epoch-making study of *Canada's Balance of Indebtedness*. His lead has been taken up by quite a number of economists who have tested the validity of the economic theory of international adjustment from the experience of their several countries. Mr. Pandit's work forms an important addition to the growing literature on this branch of applied Economics. Our author has selected India's experience during the period 1898–1913 as the subject of his study. This was a period of increased foreign borrowings by India and of expanding foreign demand for her products. It was also the period during which the Gold Exchange Standard was being gradually introduced into the country. The author had thus the opportunity of finding out not only whether the theory of international adjustment is borne out by India's experience but also of showing to what extent, if any, the process of adjustment was affected by her peculiar currency organization. An opportunity was afforded to him of studying the history of Indian currency from a new point of view.

Such a study as that carried out by Mr. Pandit regarding the interrelations of the foreign borrowings, the barter terms of trade, and the price-level of India throws important light upon the currency controversies of our country alike new and old. Thus in their study of the great rise of prices in India during the first decade of this century, critics like the late Professor Nicholson and his followers were so obsessed with the supposed imperfections of the Gold Exchange Standard as a monetary system that they attributed the rise of prices entirely to these imperfections and drawbacks and lost sight of the great importance of the changes in the volume of our foreign trade, especially of the increased volume of our exports. The errors of these critics might, however, be condoned to a considerable extent, since they were writing before the labours of Professors Taussig and Viner as well as of others showed the true relations between the position of a country in international trade and capital market and the price-level prevailing in it. Basing myself on the results and theories of these eminent writers I showed in my *Indian Currency System* that it was the increasing demand for Indian exports and the improved position of India in international trade which were in the main the ultimate causes of the rising prices of India. Mr. Pandit has worked out the topic at even greater length and with a wealth of statistical material; and he has demonstrated the bearings of the increased demand for India's exports and of her borrowings on the country's price-level at the time.

A study of Mr. Pandit's book will benefit alike the student of economic theory and one who is interested in the monetary and financial history of our country. There are notable studies in the work of India's commodity balance of trade, its balance of service transactions, and its balance of non-commercial transactions. There is a good deal that is original in these chapters as also in the examination of the amount of foreign capital invested in India. Then follows a comprehensive and careful study of the mechanism of adjustment, of the adjustment of the balance payment and changes in relative price-levels.

I can best conclude these few introductory remarks by expressing a hope that Mr. Pandit's book will secure that attention from our publicists and students of Economics which it well deserves; and that it will contribute to the clarification of ideas on important aspects of problems relating to our foreign trade and currency.

J. C. COYAJEE

BOMBAY

November 1, 1936

CONTENTS

INTRODUCTION

The possibility of applying inductive methods in co-operation with deduction to describe and explain the changes in the volume and character of international trade, the movements of price-levels, the part played by exchange rates and gold movements in the adjustment of trade balances and the reaction upon internal economic conditions of changes in international trade, has been proved by the researches in that field made by the students of Professor Taussig. The quantitative determination of the division of gains from international trade is beyond solution by either method, but here also measurement of relative changes is quite possible. For that, inductive method can be used both to test the expectations of deductive theory as to the direction of the change in the division of the gains, following upon a major disturbance in the conditions governing international trade, and given the direction of this change to measure the degree of change in the ratio in which the gains are divided.

The present study is an attempt at inductive analysis of the mechanism of adjustment of trade balances, with special reference to Indian conditions during 1898 to 1913. There are a good many reasons pointing to Indian trade history during this period as a particularly fruitful field for research. To begin with, an inductive investigation of social phenomena, in order that it may bring results of any definiteness and reliability, must confine itself to factors which in the situation studied are of sufficient importance to influence appreciably the phenomena causally related to it. If minor factors in a complex situation are investigated with the intention of measuring their effects, it is often found that their effects are so mixed up with the effects of other factors as to be completely lost in the complexity of the situation. If, therefore, we want to attempt an inductive analysis of the mechanism of adjustment of trade balances, the factors creating the trade balances must be sufficiently powerful to dominate the whole situation and there must not be any other factor besides them disturbing the process of adjustment. The period 1898 to 1913 is a period in Indian economic history conforming to these conditions:

Firstly, this period was marked by a general business prosperity all over the world punctuated by the crisis of 1907.

Secondly, the even balance between India's credit and debit international obligations which existed before 1898 was disturbed during the period by two important factors connected with the balance of payments, viz. the foreign borrowings and the increased foreign demand for India's export commodities.

Thirdly, the fluctuations in the rupee-sterling ratio which were a great disturbing factor to India's foreign trade during the eighties of the nineteenth century was absent during this period because of the introduction of the gold-exchange standard.

Out of the two factors disturbing the even balance of payment we have devoted our attention mainly to the adjustment of India's balance of indebtedness to foreign borrowings and only incidentally to the adjustment of trade balances caused by the increased foreign demand for India's export commodities. The purpose of restricting our attention mainly to the adjustment of foreign borrowings is to find out whether the mechanism of adjustment of balance of indebtedness is the same under a gold-exchange standard as under a gold standard, and, if different, how far it is different.

The study is divided into two parts. In the first part, which deals with a statistical analysis of India's annual balance of payment every year during 1898 to 1913, an attempt has been made to evaluate all the important items of payment, visible as well as invisible. The balance of payment itself has been split up into four parts, viz.: Balance of Commodity Transactions, Balance of Service Transactions, Balance of Non-Commercial Transactions, and the Balance of Indebtedness, and each part has been separately treated in detail. Finally, we have tried to verify the indirect estimate of India's balance of indebtedness with the help of all the available data bearing directly on India's foreign borrowings. For the purpose of this statistical analysis we have considered only the sea-borne foreign trade of India and ignored the transfrontier trade, which hardly comes up to 5 per cent of the former. It is necessary to state here that the estimates of different items in India's balance of payment made in this part are approximate at the most.

In the second part we have tried to find out how far the classical theory of the mechanism of adjustment of international indebtedness is borne out by Indian conditions during the period of our study. In this connection we have examined the course of India's foreign exchanges, gold movements—Council Bills—price-levels, commodity imports and exports, and barter terms of trade. However, as the behaviour of these factors during 1898 to 1913 was influenced jointly by the foreign borrowings of India and the increasing demand for her exports, it has not been possible to establish a causal relation between the behaviour of these factors and the foreign borrowings alone. Still, a partial corroboration of the classical theory of the mechanism of adjustment has been obtained.

PART I

STATISTICAL ANALYSIS

INTRODUCTORY

In order to avoid any misunderstanding we give here a brief explanation of some of the important terms used in the following pages.

A transaction which creates a pecuniary obligation on the part of a person in India towards someone outside India is called a debit transaction, and one which creates an obligation towards an Indian by a person outside India is called a credit transaction. The difference between the total of Indian credit and debit international transactions constitutes India's balance of indebtedness. If the credits exceed the debits there is a credit balance of indebtedness, and if the debits exceed the credits there is a debit balance of indebtedness. The balance of payments (assuming that all immediate obligations are immediately liquidated) represents the difference only between immediate credit and debit obligations and not the difference between all the credit and debit obligations—immediate as well as deferred—which we designate as the balance of indebtedness. If some of the transactions are on a deferred payment basis, as is generally the case, there may be a debit balance of indebtedness at the same time that there is a credit balance of payments and vice versa. The commodity balance of trade, the balance of service transactions, and the balance of non-commercial transactions represent, respectively, the differences between the imports and exports of commodities, the imports and exports of services, and the inward and outward remittances on non-commercial account, irrespective in each case whether or not the obligations created thereby are immediate or deferred. The total of these three balances equals the balance of international indebtedness, which for any period is equivalent to the difference between the total foreign loans and the total foreign borrowings of a country during that period.

In this part of the study, the commodity balance of trade,

the balance of service transactions, and the balance of non-commercial transactions for India are first estimated for each year during the period 1898 to 1913 and the balance of India's international indebtedness is then compiled from these partial balances. This balance of indebtedness gives an indirect estimate of the total amount of foreign capital invested in India during the period. The correctness of this indirect estimate of foreign investments in India and indirectly of the various estimates involved in calculating the partial balances is then tested by a direct estimate of the amount of foreign capital invested in India based upon the available information bearing on such investments.

CHAPTER I

INDIA'S COMMODITY BALANCE OF TRADE

THE term "Commodity Balance" means the balance or the difference between the values of import and export of goods. In ascertaining the commodity balance of a country, trade in precious metals is sometimes included in and sometimes excluded from the balance sheet, according to the purpose in view. If the balance is to be struck simply to realize the extent of immediate obligations during a particular year, which is not liquidated by any shipment of goods or services, the transactions in precious metals are excluded. Their main function in that case is to settle the balance of immediate obligations in respect of commodities and services which is to be ascertained. When, however, the purpose is to find out the balance of all the obligations, immediate as well as deferred, which is not liquidated even by means of gold and silver, the trade in precious metals is invariably included in the balance sheet of commodity transactions.

This part of our study is entirely concerned with a detailed analysis of our balance sheet and the evaluation of various items entering the account of our international credits and debits. To us, therefore, it does not matter whether in the commodity balance of trade we include transactions in precious metals or not. However, there is a reason which suggests their inclusion. Since the closure of Indian mints to the free coinage of silver in 1893, imports and exports of precious metals (barring the coins, which form a very small proportion of the total transactions) have been pure commodity transactions, having no direct relation to the currency circulation in the country.

Information about the annual foreign trade of India in goods and treasure is available in the statistical publications of the Government of India relating to the trade of British India. These exclude from their purview the trade of French and Portuguese India, the ports of the Indian Native States, and the small Indian Dependencies.[1] But the foreign sea-borne trade of British Indian ports represents "not merely the trade of the territory directly under British administration, but rather the trade of the whole of India and Burma, including the Indian States."

In order to be able to understand and interpret the figures relating to our sea-borne trade which are given in the various statistical publications of the Government, it is essential to know the method of their compilation, the system of computing their values, the items they include and exclude, and the unit of period for which they are made up.

THE INDIAN COMMERCE STATISTICS

(1) *Method of Compilation*

The statistical data for the foreign trade of British India are first collected by the Customs Department and are based upon values declared by importers and exporters. The declarations in the "Bills of Entry" and "Shipping Bills" are, however, checked by Customs officials before they are recorded for statistical purposes. The figures thus collected are reworked by the Commercial Intelligence Department into other forms and are published with elaborate classification in the *Annual Statement of the Sea-borne Trade and Navigation of British India* for fiscal years ending March 31st, and with less detail in the *Accounts relating to the Sea-borne Trade and Navigation of British India* for the calendar year. Since April 1, 1911, statistics of imports have included all goods landed on Indian shores, even though some of them might be imported for re-export; the imports are credited to the country which

[1] League of Nations' *Memorandum on Balance of Payments and Foreign Trade Balances, 1910–23*, vol. ii, p. 317.

sends them directly to India without any break of journey, except for change of conveyance or route. The country concerned may not necessarily be the producer of the goods; it is sufficient if it owns them at the time they are exported.[1] In the case of exports a distinction is made between exports of Indian merchandise—goods produced or manufactured in India—and exports of foreign merchandise, i.e. goods imported from foreign countries for re-export.[2] The exports and re-exports are both credited to India and debited against the countries of final destination irrespective of their possessing a sea-borne trade or not. The double entry of re-exported goods, first in the statement of imports and then in the statement of exports, prevents them from having any serious effect on India's commodity balance of trade, the accretion or decretion of values of the re-exported goods due to a change in their prices in the interval between their import into India and their re-export from it and also due to the addition of warehousing charges being very small. In addition to the figures thus collected from the declarations of importers and exporters, articles imported and despatched by parcel post and registered letter post are also adequately recorded though they are not classified according to the nature of their contents; they appear under the general heading of Postal Articles.

Prior to April 1, 1911, imports and exports were credited to the countries in which the port of shipment for imports and the port of discharge for exports were situated. It was

[1] "The country of consignment is defined as 'that from which the goods have come whether by land and sea or by sea only, without interruption of transit save in the course of transhipment or transfer from one means of conveyance to another.' " *Accounts relating to the Sea-borne Trade of India.* Introductory Notes.

[2] "The country of final destination is defined as 'that to which goods exported from India are intended to pass whether by sea and land or by sea only, without interruption of transit save in the course of transhipment or transfer from one means of conveyance to another.' " Ibid.

natural, therefore, that countries like Switzerland, which had no sea-borne trade whatsoever, never made their appearance in the Indian statistical tables. "Moreover, although the port of discharge for exports was taken to mean the final port in cases of transhipment, the port of shipment for imports was in cases of transhipment taken to be the port of transhipment and not the original port of shipment except in those cases, by no means general, where a through bill of lading had been granted."[1]

(2) *Methods of Computing Values*

In computing the values of Indian imports and exports the methods used are those which are common to the majority of commercial countries in the world. Imports are valued on their arrival at the port of entry, freight, insurance, and transport charges being included, i.e. on what is technically known as the c.i.f. basis (c.i.f. = cost, insurance, and freight). On the other hand, these charges are excluded in computing the values of our exports, which are therefore said to represent f.o.b. values—f.o.b. meaning free on board ship. The values recorded by the Customs Department in India for statistical purposes are the actual market values which are arrived at by deducting from the wholesale cash price of the goods concerned the genuine trade discount which the goods of the like kind are likely to command, when sold at the time and place of importation or exportation as the case may be. No other abatement or deduction in their values is effected unless it be the amount of duties payable in the case of imports. When, however, the wholesale cash price of a particular commodity, imported or exported, is not ascertainable, the commodity being altogether new to the market, the recorded value represents the cost at which goods of the like kind and quality could be delivered at such place with the necessary modifica-

[1] *Accounts relating to the Sea-borne Trade of India.* Introductory Notes.

tions in respect of duties and trade discounts. These recorded values do not necessarily represent the actual cash prices receivable or payable by India on her exports or imports.

The existence of a higher level of import duties induces the importer to understate the value of his goods. (The higher the level of import tariff the larger the percentage of undervaluation which is likely.) The League of Nations in calculating the balance of payments of different countries allows an extra 5 per cent for the possible undervaluation of imports in this manner. But we must remember that the League's calculations refer to post-war years when the general level of import duties in the world was fairly high. On the other hand, the level of duties in India during the period of our study was much lower and hence a much smaller allowance should be made for the undervaluation of her imports. We have in our study corrected the recorded values of Indian imports by making an allowance of 1 per cent for undervaluation.

(3) *Omissions and Inclusions*

In every country the recorded statistics of imports and exports take account of certain articles which, according to the strict theory of international trade, ought to be totally excluded, while others which ought to be included are ignored. This is due to the "conditions peculiar to the trade" of different countries or the result of some long-standing practice in the department responsible for the collection of statistics. We must therefore search out the unscientific inclusions and omissions of this character in the statistics of commodity imports and exports of India and make allowance for them in striking the commodity balance.

One such item is "settlers' effects." The value of all dutiable articles found in the luggage of passengers is recorded along with the imports of commodities. But these articles move with their owners and do not give rise to any international obligations. Again, though the movements of dutiable luggage apparently resemble capital movements, they are really quite different because they do not necessitate payment of interest and repayment of the principal. Hence the value of "settlers' effects" included without justification in the statistics of commodity imports must be deducted. On the other hand, the "fish caught in extra-territorial waters and landed direct from the fishing-grounds," imports of ships except those for inland or harbour navigation and the imports of diamonds and other precious stones,[1] which are not reckoned in our trade statistics, must receive due consideration in India's commodity balance of trade. However, as neither of the items enumerated above can be evaluated even approximately and as they are comparatively insignificant in value, we shall ignore them.

(4) *Selection of the Year*

For the sake of this study, which comprises the pre-war period of the Gold-Exchange Standard, we have selected the Indian fiscal year as our basis. This is mainly because the major portion of Indian statistics is published for the fiscal year only, and as we may have to correlate our trade figures with other economic data, which are also published for the fiscal year, it will save us a good deal of trouble if we choose the fiscal year rather than the calendar year.[2]

(5) *Accuracy of Indian Commerce Statistics*

We have now examined the basis of our commercial statistics and the system of their collection and tabulation. We shall

[1] G. Findlay Shirras, "India's Real Balance of Trade." A paper read before the Seventh Indian Economic Conference. *Proceedings*, p. 72.

[2] Wherever it will be necessary to adjust calendar year figures to the fiscal year basis the adjustment will be brought about on the assumption of equal monthly distribution of the data for the whole of the calendar year.

next see how far they are accurate and what are their drawbacks. In the first place, our statistical records are often faulty. In many cases the figures for a particular item do not agree with the figures for the same item presented in a later issue of the same publication. The discrepancies, though not big enough to upset rough calculations, are sufficiently embarrassing to an honest researcher. In a situation like this we have to rely on our discretion for the selection of proper figures, which leaves a margin, however small, for error. The second and the greatest defect of our commercial statistics is their lack of uniformity. Even if the frequent changes in the system of classifying the traded goods with which we are not immediately concerned be ignored, the changing monetary unit in which values are expressed is extremely embarrassing. Till 1873–74 the values of imports and exports were expressed in pounds. From 1873–74 to 1898–99 they were recorded in rupees. There was a reversion to the sterling basis in the latter year when again the pound was selected as the unit of recorded values and remained as such till the year 1913–14. Since that year the rupee has been used as the unit of value. Fortunately, however, these changes do not affect the period of our study 1898–1913. During these years all foreign trade values were, as we have noted, recorded in pounds and we have only to convert them into rupees to make them directly comparable with other figures. Thirdly, sometimes even the columns of the statistical tables are not properly captioned and footnotes are not given where they are absolutely necessary to avoid misunderstanding and wrong interpretation. In spite of these defects, however, we have to rely on official statistics as the only source of our information, allowing for their inaccuracies and inconsistencies before we draw important conclusions.

Table I represents the balance of transactions in merchandise, including Government stores.

Statistics regarding the imports and exports of treasure

are adequate enough. Imports and exports of gold and silver, both as bullion and coin, are separately given in addition to the transactions in currency notes. Under the Gold-Exchange

TABLE I

BALANCE OF MERCHANDISE TRANSACTIONS, EXCLUDING PRECIOUS METALS BUT INCLUDING GOVERNMENT STORES AND POSTAL ARTICLES

*(In Lakhs of Rupees)**

Year	*Imports of Merchandise*†	*Imports of Merchandise Corrected for Under Assessment*‡	*Exports of Merchandise*
1898–99	7,210	7,282	11,280
1899–00	7,530	7,605	10,909
1900–01	8,089	8,170	10,770
1901–02	8,873	8,962	12,489
1902–03	8,582	8,668	12,939
1903–04	9,259	9,352	15,352
1904–05	10,441	10,545	15,772
1905–06	12,211	12,333	16,184
1906–07	11,724	11,841	17,703
1907–08	13,664	13,801	17,719
1908–09	12,878	13,007	15,314
1909–10	12,265	12,388	18,799
1910–11	13,370	13,504	20,996
1911–12	14,405	14,549	22,798
1912–13	16,663	16,830	24,622
1913–14	19,131	19,322	24,901

* Pound values converted into rupee values at the rate of 1s. 4d. to the rupee.

† Import values presented in these columns include freight and insurance charges.

‡ One per cent of the value of total commodity imports (excluding precious metals) has been added to allow for under-assessment.

Standard gold was available to the people only to settle their foreign obligations if need be and not for internal transactions. Similar was the case with silver bullion. As mints were closed to the free coinage of silver, people could no longer convert their silver bars into rupees and hence for all practical purposes silver came to be regarded as no better than an ordinary marketable commodity. It was, however, quite different with sovereigns, half-sovereigns, rupees, and the currency notes which were imported or exported. During the period of our study all these currencies were legal tender in India and therefore their inward and outward movements must have had some effect on prices and consequently on trade. But as imports and exports of legal tender currencies were a very small proportion of the total imports and exports of treasure, and as the amount of sovereigns in circulation as medium of exchange was not large their effect on prices was imperceptible. The total recorded excess of imports of treasure over its exports during 1898–99 to 1913–14 amounted to 40,806 lakhs of rupees. As gold coins were scarcely used as medium of exchange, they along with gold bullion should have swelled the gold reserves of the Government and the banks, as in Canada during the period 1900 to 1913. Silver should have gone to the market as a commodity and rupees and notes entered into day to day circulation. These inferences, however, are not borne out by actual facts. The increase in the gold reserves of the Government and of the banks as compared with the total net imports of the yellow metal during the period was very small. This important difference between Canada and India in the matter of absorbing gold is due to the difference in the agencies controlling its imports and exports in the two countries. In Canada most of the imports and exports of gold are managed by a centralized organization. The reserve system for Canadian currency was centralized, while banking was in the hands of less than twenty-five banks.[1] In India imports of gold were largely on private account, which in the absence of a centralized banking organization and the prevalence of the hoarding habit among the people disappeared into sinks. This explains why the gold reserves of the Government and of the banks in

[1] J. Viner, *Canada's Balance of International Indebtedness*, p. 15.

India do not show a proportionate increase with the total net imports of precious metals.

Table II shows India's balance of transactions in precious metals.

Now, it might appear at first sight that given the balances of transactions in merchandise and treasure, calculation of

TABLE II

BALANCE OF TRANSACTIONS IN TREASURE

(In lakhs of Rupees)

Year	Imports* Government Account	Imports* Private Account	Imports* Total	Exports Government Account	Exports Private Account	Exports Total
1898–99	1	1,789	1,790		741	741
1899–00	1	2,096	2,097		795	795
1900–01	812	1,646	2,458	675	748	1,423
1901–02	94	1,965	2,059	300	847	1,147
1902–03	13	2,525	2,538	85	869	954
1903–04	658	3,194	3,852	689	804	1,493
1904–05	648	3,302	3,950	844	809	1,653
1905–06	1,072	2,092	3,164	102	1,444	1,546
1906–07	1,737	2,720	4,457		571	571
1907–08	946	3,282	4,228		545	545
1908–09	11	2,262	2,273	36	595	631
1909–10	9	3,742	3,751		638	638
1910–11	7	3,966	3,973		712	712
1911–12	5	5,341	5,346		1,037	1,037
1912–13	1,063	5,120	6,183	358	705	1,063
1913–14	682	3,662	4,344	3	705	708

* Import values presented in these columns include freight and insurance charges.

the commodity balance of trade is only a step further. But this is not so. As we have already seen, the recorded values of our imports include freight and insurance charges in addition to their cost prices. In a purely commodity balance of trade, however, payments for invisible items like freight and insurance, which are in the nature of services, ought not to figure. The values of these items, therefore, will have to be deducted from the recorded values of our imports before we can strike a pure commodity balance.

Here we come face to face with a great difficulty. No separate statistics of freight and insurance charges payable by India are published. In fact, no country in the world publishes them. Economists and statisticians,[1] however, have evolved a few indirect methods of ascertaining the freight charges earned or the freight bill paid by a country. We shall examine these methods and see how far they are available for ascertaining freight charges paid on Indian imports during 1898–1913.

METHODS OF ASCERTAINING FREIGHT CHARGES

The first method is based on the reasoning that "since the imports and exports of the whole world are, for the most part, the same goods valued at the point of arrival and departure respectively, the excess of value of imports should give a rough measure of the difference of valuation due to the cost of ocean carriage, including freight, insurance, and other charges."[2] Sir Robert Giffen makes use of this method in his paper on *The Use of Import and Export Statistics*, read before the Royal Statistical Society. Giffen estimates the excess of the value of world imports over world exports. This sum is assumed to be equal to the freight and insurance charges paid on the world trade. Making a further assumption that the freight and insurance charges on a country's import trade are the same proportion of the value of its imports as the total of the world's freight and insurance charges are to that of total world imports, the freight and insurance charges payable by any country can be easily ascertained.

The implicit assumption of this method is that all import.

[1] Sir R. Giffen, "The Use of Import and Export Statistics," *Journal of the Royal Statistical Society*, June 1882.

C. K. Hobson, *Export of Capital*, "Measurement of the Balance of Trade," *Economica*, May 1921.

J. Viner, *Canada's Balance of International Indebtedness*.

G. L. Wood, *Borrowing and Business in Australia*.

[2] Edgar Crammond, *The British Shipping Industry*, p. 17. Quoted by J. Viner, op. cit., p. 65.

values are recorded c.i.f. and all export values f.o.b. in statistics of world commerce. In the case of many countries, however, this is not true. For example, in the United States of America, Canada, British South Africa, Cuba, Mexico, and Philippines import statistics are based upon f.o.b. values. Naturally, the excess of world imports over world exports in value, will not include the freight and insurance charges on the import trade of these countries, which constitutes a considerable proportion of the world's import trade. Thus the accuracy of the primary data used in this method will suffer. Secondly, prior to the relevant publications of the League of Nations, there was no authoritative compilation of statistics relating to the world's import and export trade, which is also a great handicap in the use of this method. Thirdly, a great many countries compile their trade statistics on the basis of official valuations which are arbitrary in character. The amount of error that creeps into the primary data from this fact could have been largely reduced if the same method of "official valuations" was applied to both imports and exports. But that is not always the case, e.g. in Greece import figures are based on an official valuation made in 1899, while exports are valued at current average prices.[1] In addition to these divergent practices, the adoption of different fiscal years and of different definitions of imports and exports by different countries for statistical purposes render consolidation of commercial data for the world as a whole extremely difficult. But even if all these drawbacks could be ignored the application of a world percentage of freight and insurance charges to individual countries which differ widely from one another in the degree to which their trade is bulky or comes from close-by regions or is frontier traffic, has no justification whatsoever.

The second method is to ascertain the receipts per ton of shipping for foreign Mercantile Marines, for which official

[1] C. K. Hobson, "Measurement of the Balance of Trade," *Economica*, June 1921, p. 133.

statistics are published in Sweden and Denmark, or for those shipping companies in the country itself which publish similar information, and to deduce therefrom the receipts of the country's aggregate tonnage engaged in foreign trade. This method can be used to calculate the earnings from shipping of a country which possesses Mercantile Marine. In the case of Great Britain it has been successfully used, because she has the largest Mercantile Marine in the world. But our objective is to estimate the freight and other charges paid on her import trade by India, which does not possess any Mercantile Marine. We can, however, assume that the earnings of foreign shipping engaged in India's international trade are, after certain deductions, equal to the freight and insurance charges on that trade. But this would not help us very much. In the first place the earnings per ton of foreign shipping for which figures are available are the averages of earnings made over all sea-routes. Secondly, even if we assume that the earnings per ton on Indian trade were equal to these averages, we shall get composite figures for receipts on import and export trade, while we really want to have the figures for our import trade only.

A third method of estimating the freight earnings or payments of a country is to consider all the shipping tonnage engaged in her foreign trade as time-chartered and add to the charter money the charterer's disbursements for bunker coal and port dues. The aggregate of these charges would be the gross earnings or gross payments of a country on account of freight. If the foreign trade is carried in foreign as well as national bottoms, adjustments will have to be made according to the proportion of foreign and national shipping. The amount of charter money can be calculated from the published market rates, and expenditure on bunkers can be reckoned on the basis of the average consumption of coal per ton of shipping. The most serious drawback of this method is that charter rates are available only for tramps. Liners which sail at regular intervals, which have a faster speed and which carry a considerable proportion of freight, naturally earn more. But allowance for the superior earnings of the liners cannot be made by means of any known method. Another objection to this method, which is a corollary to the first, is that "movements of tramp freights are not a satisfactory index to movements of other shipping rates." The earnings of tramp vessels are more fluctuating than the earnings of other kinds of vessels.

For India this method has been used by Mr. S. N. Haji (Manager, Scindia Steam Navigation Company, Ltd., Rangoon) to estimate freight charges on India's imports and exports in the year 1921–22. It is, however, not possible for us to use this method for the present study. Charter rates (or the index of charter rates) for tramps engaged in India's import trade during the period 1898–99 to 1913–14 are not available. Moreover, for reasons already stated, the method is theoretically defective.

There is a fourth method which was invented by the British Board of Trade for ascertaining the percentage increase in British shipping earnings between 1913 and 1920.[1] The important ocean trade routes of the world were grouped into thirteen main routes and the distribution of British shipping on these routes was ascertained. Then from the published rates of freight for important commodities the approximate receipts for each route were calculated. But this method also cannot be of any use to us as the distribution of shipping on the Indian trade route, which is considered as one of the main routes, cannot be ascertained for the individual years covered by the period of our study.

PROFESSOR VINER'S METHOD

J. Viner in his critical study of *Canada's Balance of International Indebtedness* has used a different method for calculating the freight charges payable by Canada.[2] He collects the average freight rates per ton, from United Kingdom to Montreal, on

[1] *The Board of Trade Journal*, February 3, 1921, p. 116.
[2] J. Viner, *Canada's Balance of International Indebtedness*, p. 68.

iron and steel manufactures and cotton textiles for a normal year in the period of his study. He assumes these two groups of commodities to represent the bulky and light articles respectively, comprising Canada's import trade with Great Britain, and computes the percentage of freight charges to their import values per ton. Next, the actual proportions of bulky and light articles in the imports are obtained and the crude percentages are weighted and averaged. This weighted percentage is then applied to the total value of Canada's imports from Great Britain and the total absolute freight charges are obtained. To use this *ad valorem* percentage for the other years making up his period, he makes adjustments for changes in freight rates, prices, and the proportion of bulky and light commodities from year to year. This method has been slightly elaborated and applied to Australian conditions by G. L. Wood. The improvement consists in the selection of a large number of articles to represent the import trade, instead of a group or two as done by Viner. "The device finally selected consisted of taking the analysis of imports into classes made by the Commonwealth Statistician, and loading for a normal year a sample cargo representative of all lines imported in a typical ship of 15,000 tons displacement. . . . For a normal cargo composed in this way it was calculated that the value at prices prevailing in 1908 was approximately £230,000, upon which the freight payable at 1908 rates would amount to about £15,000, i.e. 6 per cent."[1]

This method of ascertaining freight charges is best suited to the Indian situation and is likely to give more reliable results than any of the other methods discussed before. We have already rejected these either on the ground that their bases are faulty or that they are inapplicable to Indian conditions. So by a process of elimination we come to select the method used by J. Viner. But before proceeding to utilize it we shall have to make certain assumptions. We assume that the *ad*

[1] G. L. Wood, *Business and Borrowing in Australia*, p. 147.

valorem percentage of freight charges to the value of our import trade with Great Britain is applicable to our import trade with all countries. This assumption can be justified on the ground that India's import trade with Great Britain during the period under consideration was more than 60 per cent of her total import trade. We assume, further, that the freight rates on imports of cotton manufactures, chemicals, and iron and steel goods can be made use of to represent the rates on imports of important groups of commodities which covered the whole or the major portion of India's import trade during the period. Cotton manufactures stand for all kinds of textile fabrics, which are the most important group of our imports. Chemicals fall into a category by themselves on which import freights are exceptionally high and the manufactures of iron and steel represent the heavy and bulky commodities.

Instead of strictly adhering to Viner's method and ascertaining the *ad valorem* percentage of freight charges to import values for a normal year we shall calculate the average of the *ad valorem* percentage of freight charges to import values for the years 1904–5, 1905–6, 1906–7.[1] This departure from the original method has been made to ensure greater accuracy in results. The next step is to collect information on the following points:

(i) Average freight rates per ton on the representative commodity groups from the United Kingdom to Bombay and Calcutta, the chief ports of import in India, for the years 1904–5, 1905–6, and 1906–7.

(ii) Average import values per ton of the commodity groups for the three years.

(iii) Conversion rate from measurement to weight basis for cotton manufactures, the import values of which are given per yard and freight rates per ton.

[1] Instead of one normal year we have taken three normal years.

(iv) The respective shares of our import trade represented by the three groups of commodities during the three years.

The data for freight charges and import values are available in K. L. Dutta's report on Indian prices.

For computing the conversion rate of cotton goods from measurement to weight basis we have to rely on information collected from different sources. The *Statistical Abstracts for the United Kingdom* supplies figures for the annual exports of cotton piece-goods in yards only. Professor J. W. Daniels and J. J. Jewkes, in an article in the *Economic Journal*, give the average of piece-goods exported by Great Britain during 1909–10 to 1913–14 in metric tons.[1] Hence by calculating a similar average of piece-goods exports in terms of yards we can get the rate of conversion for the piece-goods exported by the United Kingdom during those years. From this we can deduce the conversion rate for India.[2] About 90 per cent of the cotton piece-goods imported by India during the period under study were of British manufacture. But the goods taken by India, as shown by the post-war particulars, must have been substantially lighter, somewhat wider on average, and of cheaper grade than the mass of other exports.[3] Making allowance for

[1] Professor J. W. Daniels and J. J. Jewkes, "The Crisis in the Lancashire Cotton Industry," *Economic Journal*, March 1927.

[2] *Statistical Abstracts for the United Kingdom.* Average exports of piece-goods by the United Kingdom during the period 1909–13 = 6,476 million yards. *Economic Journal*, March 1927, p. 39, average exports of piece-goods by the United Kingdom during the period 1909–13 = 526,837 metric tons.

1 metric ton = 12,292 yards.
i.e. 1 lb. = 5·6 yards.

There are two assumptions made here which might be stated: (*a*) that the average for 1903–13 applies for the earlier years; (*b*) the average for all British exports applies to exports to India.

[3] A. W. Flux, "British Export Trade," *Economic Journal*, December 1926, p. 558.

this factor, the conversion rate for cotton piece-goods imported in India is assumed to be 1 lb. = 5·4 yards.

All the other necessary data for computing the *ad valorem* percentage of freight charges to import values according to the method adopted by us are presented in Table III.

TABLE III

IMPORT VALUES AND FREIGHT RATES

(*Average of three years* 1904–05 *to* 1906–07)

Commodity Group	*Average Import Value* per Ton* *Rs.*	*Average Freight Rate per Ton†* *Rs.*	*Percentage of Freight Charges to Import Values*	*Average Weights*	*Final Percentage (weighted)*
Cotton manufactures	1,701	10·75	0·6	31	18·6
Chemicals	182	27·5	15·0	2	33·0
Iron and Steel Manufactures‡ ..	—	—	6·2	67	415·4
					467·0
					4·7 per cent.

* K. L. Dutta: *An Enquiry into the Rise of Prices in India*, vol. iii, p. 486—Values c.i.f.

† K. L. Dutta: Ibid., vol. iii, p. 484—Values c.i.f.

‡ The *ad valorem* percentage of freight charges to import values in the case of iron and steel manufactures relates to galvanized plates, sheets and plates, steel bars, and railway plant and rolling stock.

The average of the weighted *ad valorem* percentage of freight charges to import values for the three years 1904–5, 1905–6, 1906–7 has now been calculated. To apply this percentage to the other years during the period 1898–99 to 1913–14 we have to take into account the changes in the relative weights of representative commodity groups, freight rates, and prices every year.

The weights of representative commodity groups and the corresponding *ad valorem* percentages of freight charges to import values are given in Table IV.

The changes in the weights as we see are not considerable and consequently they are not expected to affect the *ad valorem* percentage of freight charges in any way seriously. But the case is different with the other two factors to be considered.

K. L. Dutta's report on Indian prices gives freight quotations on all the important commodities imported on Government

TABLE IV

WEIGHTS OF REPRESENTATIVE COMMODITY GROUPS AND THE AD VALOREM PERCENTAGES OF FREIGHT CHARGES*

Year	*Fabrics*	*Chemicals*	*Heavy Commodities*	*Percentage of Freight Charges*
1898–99	34	2·8	63	4·5
1899–00	35	2·7	62	4·5
1900–01	33	2·3	65	4·6
1901–02	34	2·5	63	4·5
1902–03	31	2·7	66	4·7
1903–04	28	2·4	70	4·9
1904–05	32	2.2	66	4·6
1905–06	34	2·3	64	4·5
1906–07	27	2·0	71	4·9
1907–08	30	2·0	68	4·7
1908–09	30	2·2	68	4·7
1909–10	29	2·3	69	4·8
1910–11	30	2·1	68	4·7
1911–12	29	2·0	69	4·8
1912–13	31	1·8	67	4·6
1913–14	32	1·9	68	4·7

* Compiled from the *Statistical Abstracts for British India.*

account. We assume that these quotations are applicable to the imports of similar merchandise on private account. This assumption cannot be seriously questioned, as the Government are not reported to receive any special concessions in freight rates. Applying these quotations to our representative commodity groups we have compiled a weighted index number of inward freights. However, these freight quotations are available only for the period 1901–2 to 1912–13. For the years prior to 1901–2 we shall use the Board of Trade's outward freight index, as has been done by J. Viner when faced with a similar difficulty.[1] Then there remains the year 1913–14, for which we shall have the Australian freight index.[2] The reason for selecting Australia and not Canada or any other country for supplying us the index of freight rates is quite obvious. Australia lies at the extremity of the same ocean trade route which connects India with the United Kingdom and the composition of her import and export trade and of the shipping engaged in it are similar to those of India. The freight indices of the Board of Trade and of Australia have been adjusted to the Indian fiscal year basis to incorporate them into the Indian freight index. The adjustment is made on the assumption of equal monthly distribution. All the three indices have been readjusted to the average of three years, 1904–5 to 1906–7, as the basis and the new index represents the movement of inward Indian freight rates during the period of our study.

As regards the index of prices in Great Britain we shall use the Board of Trade's figures. Like the freight index this index also has been adjusted to the fiscal year basis and readjusted to the average of three years 1904–5, 1905–6, and 1906–7.

The *ad valorem* percentage of freight charges to total imports as computed in Table IV after making allowance for changes in the weights of the representative commodity groups, "multiplied for each year by the freight index and also by the reciprocal of the price index, will give the *ad valorem* percentage of freight charges to imports for each year in the period." The final calculation of freight charges payable by India on her imports is presented in Table V.

The irregular movement of freight rates indicated by the freight index is largely due to the prevalence of tramps in the Indian Ocean. At the beginning of the twentieth century

[1] J. Viner, *Canada's Balance of International Indebtedness, 1900–13*, p. 74.

[2] G. L. Wood, *Borrowing and Business in Australia.*

freight rates were unusually high because of the Boer War, but they declined sharply after the conclusion of the war and did not recover till after 1906.[1]

TABLE V

FREIGHT PAYMENTS BY INDIA

Year	*Imports Rs. 1,00,000*	*Percentage of Freight Charges allowing for Weights*	*Freight Index**	*Price Index†*	*Percentage of Freight Charges to Imports*	*Freight Payments by India‡ Rs. 1,00,000*
1898–99	9,072	4·5	1,158§	936	5·4	471
1899–00	9,702	4·5	1,212§	949	5·9	553
1900–01	10,628	4·6	1,231	948	5·5	567
1901–02	11,021	4·5	1,503	973	6·6	706
1902–03	11,206	4·7	1,368	979	6·6	720
1903–04	13,204	4·9	1,069	1,001	5·4	695
1904–05	14,495	4·6	1,057	988	5·0	707
1905–06	15,497	4·5	1,194	989	5·4	818
1906–07	16,298	4·9	748	1,023	3·4	542
1907–08	18,029	4·7	861	1,055	3·8	671
1908–09	15,280	4·7	1,234	1,037	5·6	838
1909–10	16,139	4·8	977	1,058	4·3	680
1910–11	17,477	4·7	892	1,097	3·8	648
1911–12	19,895	4·8	1,059	1,116	4·3	829
1912–13	23,013	4·6	1,284	1,159	5·0	1,127
1913–14	23,666	4·7	1,431‖	1,173	5·6	1,299

* 1900–01 to 1912–13 compiled from K. L. Dutta's *Report on Indian Prices*, weighted and adjusted to the average of 1904–05, 1905–06, and 1906–07.

† W. T. Layton, *An Introduction to the Study of Prices*, adjusted to the average of 1904–05, 1905–06, and 1906–07 basis.

‡ For calculating freight payments the value of re-exports has been deducted from the total value of imports.

§ Compiled from the Board of Trade Freight Index adjusted to the Indian Fiscal Year basis and to the average of 1904–05, 1905–06, and 1906–07.

‖ Australian Freight Index adjusted to the fiscal year basis and to the average of 1904–05, 1905–06, and 1906–07.

METHOD OF ASCERTAINING INSURANCE CHARGES, ETC.

In addition to freight charges, insurance and other commission charges have also to be deducted from the c.i.f. import values before we can strike a pure commodity balance of trade for

[1] *The Economist*, February 16, 1901, "Commercial History and Review of 1900": "Outward freights to the East were most favourably affected by the demands of our Government necessitating their paying good rates to the Cape for prompt tonnage."

TABLE VI

India's Commodity Balance of Trade

(In lakhs of rupees)

	Imports				
Year	*Commodities**	*Treasure*†	*Total Imports c.i.f. (I + II)*	*Freight Charges on Imports*‡	*Insurance and other Commission Charges on Imports*
	I	II	III	IV	V
1898–99	7,282	1,790	9,072	471	136
1899–00	7,605	2,097	9,702	553	145
1900–01	8,170	2,458	10,628	567	159
1901–02	8,962	2,059	11,021	706	165
1902–03	8,668	2,538	11,206	720	168
1903–04	9,352	3,852	13,204	695	198
1904–05	10,545	3,950	14,495	707	217
1905–06	12,333	3,164	15,497	818	232
1906–07	11,841	4,457	16,298	542	244
1907–08	13,801	4,228	18,029	671	270
1908–09	13,007	2,273	15,280	838	229
1909–10	12,388	3,751	16,139	680	242
1910–11	13,504	3,973	17,477	648	262
1911–12	14,549	5,346	19,895	829	298
1912–13	16,830	6,183	23,013	1,127	345
1913–14	19,322	4,344	23,666	1,299	354

* Supra, Table I. † Supra, Table II. ‡ Supra, Table V.

TABLE VI—*continued*

INDIA'S COMMODITY BALANCE OF TRADE

(*In lakhs of rupees*)

Imports		Exports			
Total Freight and Insurance Charges, etc. (IV + V)	*Net Imports of Commodities and Treasure (III − VI)*	*Commodities**	*Treasure†*	*Total Exports (VIII + IX)*	*Commodity Balance of Trade (X − VII) Credit*
VI	VII	VIII	IX	X	XI
607	8,465	11,280	741	12,021	3,556
698	9,004	10,909	795	11,704	2,700
726	9,902	10,770	1,423	12,193	2,291
871	10,150	12,489	1,147	13,636	3,486
888	10,318	12,939	954	13,893	3,575
893	12,311	15,352	1,493	16,845	4,534
924	13,571	15,772	1,653	17,425	3,854
1,050	14,447	16,184	1,546	17,730	3,283
786	15,512	17,703	571	18,274	2,762
941	17,088	17,719	545	18,264	1,176
1,067	14,213	15,314	631	15,945	1,732
922	15,217	18,799	638	19,437	4,220
910	16,567	20,996	712	21,708	5,141
1,127	18,768	22,798	1,037	23,835	5,067
1,472	21,541	24,622	1,063	25,685	4,144
1,653	22,013	24,901	708	25,609	3,596

India. To evaluate these items we shall have to resort to the percentage method which we criticize elsewhere.[1] But freight rates are determined by factors which are almost independent of the value of goods transported. A change in any of these factors is likely to affect the freight rate and consequently its relation to the value of commodities, and we show that these factors are always in a flux. Moreover, even if freight rates remain constant, fluctuations in the prices of commodities are sure to affect percentage of freight charges to import or export values. In short, a freight percentage is a function of two factors which are subject to independent changes; and hence it cannot be the same for any two years except by accident. In the case of insurance and other commission charges, however, the situation is different. They are mainly related to the values of commodities and the rates are quoted as percentages of these values. These rates were more or less constant during the period of our study.[2] Sir Robert Giffen in the paper already referred to estimated that insurance and other commission charges amounted to 2·5 per cent of the value of British exports and imports in the year 1882. From careful inquiries this percentage has been reduced to 1·5 in the case of India.[3] Applying this percentage to Indian imports we calculate the insurance and other commission charges payable on account of commercial services.

The final calculation of India's commodity balance of trade is presented in Table VI.

[1] See Appendix I, p. 195.

[2] *The Economist*, February 18, 1905, "The Commercial and Economic Review."

[3] League of Nations' *Memorandum on Balance of Payments and Foreign Trade Balances, 1910-23*, vol. i, p. 20.

CHAPTER II

BALANCE OF SERVICE TRANSACTIONS

In the international transaction of a country, exchange of services is as important as the exchange of commodities. Like imports and exports of commodities, imports and exports of services create debits or credits against it or in its favour. They are often overlooked not because of their unimportance in the volume of international transactions, but chiefly because official statistics are generally limited to the movement of physical goods. Service transactions are not recorded by any country except Argentina, and this absence of records is largely responsible for the confusion that prevails about their true character. There still exists a tendency to regard payment for services as a payment for nothing. However, we consider exchange of services on a par with exchange of commodities as regards their effect on the international trade balance of a country.

In the case of India there is a large amount of invisible imports which mainly comprise commercial services. As they have to be paid for in the same way as imports of commodities we shall deal with them in this section under the following headings: freight payments, insurance and banking payments, "Home Charges," and tourists' expenditure. Statistical information on all these items except "Home Charges" is either very scanty or not at all available. Hence our estimates of their value have no claim whatsoever to exactitude.

FREIGHT PAYMENTS

Freight payments are payments for the carriage of goods from one place to another. Almost the whole of India's seaborne trade, foreign as well as coastal, was carried on British bottoms. Even the small tonnage of Indian shipping which is now engaged in our coastal trade did not exist during the period of our study. Obviously, India had to pay for the services of British shipping. However, she was not responsible for the payment of these services both on her imports and exports. In the case of foreign trade it is generally assumed that a country pays freight charges only on its imports. So far as coastal trade is concerned, our imports are exports valued c.i.f. at the ports of importation. Therefore freight payments may be supposed to have been charged either on imports or exports, but not on both. In keeping with the practice followed in the case of foreign trade we assume that they are charged on our imports. Thus on the whole India has to pay freight charges only on her imports.

FREIGHT PAYMENTS ON FOREIGN TRADE

We have already calculated the total of our freight payments on foreign imports. But it was an estimate of gross payments. A large part of these receipts must have been spent by the British Shipping Companies in India on harbour dues, for bunkers, and for the labour of loading and unloading. During the post-war year 1923–24 the amount of harbour dues paid by these companies was estimated at Rs. 2,00 lakhs.[1] Besides, a fairly large number of Indians were engaged by these companies as sailors and lascars. In the census year, 1911, the total number of Indians employed by the British Shipping Companies was 2,531: 577 in the Navigation Department, 1,363 in the Engineering Department, and 591 as cooks, stewards, etc.[2] A major portion of the wages received by them is generally spent in India. Similarly British crews during the stay of their ships in Indian harbours spend a considerable

[1] League of Nations' *Memorandum on Balance of Payments and Foreign Trade Balances, 1910–24*, vol. i.

[2] *Census of India, Report, 1911*, vol. i, p. 112.

amount of money in India. All this expenditure is ultimately met out of the gross earnings of British shipping on India's foreign imports, reducing to that extent the net amount of freight charges payable by India. In 1882 Sir Robert Giffen estimated the proportion of such expenditure at one sixth of gross receipts. On the other hand, C. K. Hobson, by analysing the "voyage accounts of two tramp steamers" plying between all the important ports of import during the period 1907–6 to 1908–9, calculates it at 30 per cent. He states, moreover, that this percentage may be assumed to remain fairly constant from year to year.[1] In view of the large number of British ships permanently located abroad since the beginning of this century, Sir Robert Giffen's estimate appears to be too low. We have therefore assumed Hobson's percentage to be true during the whole period of our study and used it to make deductions from the gross amount of freight charges payable by India.

FREIGHT PAYMENTS ON COASTAL TRADE

As in the case of freight charges on our foreign trade, there is no information whatsoever bearing directly on the freight charges payable by India for the carriage of her coastal trade. The method generally followed to ascertain these charges is based on the reasoning that as our coastal imports are exports valued c.i.f. at the port of importation, the excess of imports over exports represents freight and insurance charges. This argument, however, presupposes that the recorded imports of a particular year are the recorded exports of the same year valued c.i.f. This may not be necessarily the case. If a large consignment of goods is exported from a harbour during the third or fourth week of March, the last month of our fiscal year for which statistics are recorded, and if the ship takes

[1] Cf. "On the whole, therefore, the assumption appears justifiable that the proportion of foreign expenditure abroad is fairly constant from year to year." *The Export of Capital*, p. 173.

more than a fortnight to reach its destination, the goods, while they will be recorded as exports during that year, will not be recorded as imports during the same year. It may even be that the recorded exports of a year may never be recorded as imports and vice versa. Secondly, if the goods are exported to ports under the jurisdiction of the Native States, according to the Indian practice of recording trade statistics they would appear only on the side of coastal exports, while the exports from the Native States to British Indian ports would appear only on the side of coastal imports. If the value of exports to Native States' ports during a year is much larger than the value of imports to British India from there, the total recorded imports of that year instead of showing a surplus over the total recorded exports of the same year might even show a deficiency. In fact, this might have been the case during the year 1899–1900, for which the value of coastal imports is recorded at Rs. 4,137 lakhs and of exports at Rs. 4,339 lakhs, showing an excess of Rs. 202 lakhs over the recorded value of imports. A similar difficulty is presented by the figures of coastal imports and exports during the year 1897–8, the year immediately preceding our period. These difficulties greatly affect the applicability of the general method of ascertaining freight charges on coastal trade.

It may also be due to this slight discrepancy in the units of period covered by the recorded statistics of coastal imports and exports and to the one-sided recording of our coastal trade with the ports of the Native States, that the excess of imports over exports shows wide fluctuations. The excess of imports over exports according to the method we are discussing constitutes freight and insurance charges. Therefore the fluctuations in the excess represent fluctuations in the freight and insurance charges, which are not at all justified by the changes in freight rates.[1] The excess of coastal imports over exports and the percentage of the excess to the value of

[1] *Review of the Trade of India*, 1913–14.

coastal imports, in certain years of the period of our study, were as follows:

Year	*Coastal Imports Rs. 1,00,000*	*Coastal Exports Rs. 1,00,000*	*Excess of Imports over Exports Rs. 1,00,000*	*Percentage of the Excess to Coastal Imports*
1902–03	4,025	3,824	201	5
1903–04	4,268	3,924	344	8
1904–05	4,521	4,410	111	2
1905–06	5,050	5,009	41	1
1906–07	5,705	5,335	370	6
1912–13	6,702	6,434	268	4
1913–14	7,125	6,308	817	10

The percentage of the excess, i.e. the percentage of freight and insurance charges to the value of imports, seems to have been at almost every figure between 1 to 10 during the period 1902–3 to 1913–14. It was changing every year except during the brief interval of 1906–7 to 1912–13, when it was more or less constant, and the changes were very sweeping. The freight percentage was 8 in 1903–4. It came down to 2 with a bump the very next year. Again in the year 1905–6 the percentage figure stood at 1 but rose to 6 in 1906–7. Such abrupt changes in the freight percentage, in spite of very slight variations in the coastal freight rates[1] and in the character of freights earned, are sufficient in themselves to discredit the method of calculating the freight charges which equate these to the excess of coastal imports over exports.

Mr. S. N. Haji has used another method to calculate the freight bill payable by India on her coastal trade.[2] For the year 1921–22, to which his calculations refer, Haji ascertains the average freight rates per ton for the main commodities carried along the Indian coast. From these various averages he obtains an all India average. Multiplying the total amount of cargo carried coastwise by this average freight rate he finally arrives at the earnings of British shipping engaged in Indian

[1] *Review of the Trade of India, 1913–14.*
[2] S. N. Haji, *Economics of Shipping*, p. 320.

coastal trade. However, the data obtained by Haji for the year 1921–22 are not available for the period of our study and hence his method cannot be made use of by us.

Therefore, in the absence of a method which can give a reliable estimate of our freight charges on coastal trade we have had resort to a very rough calculation. Though coastal imports during a year may not necessarily be the coastal exports of the same year valued c.i.f., it may fairly be assumed that the total amount of coastal imports during a long period of years do represent the total of coastal exports during the same period valued c.i.f. The longer the period the lesser the percentage of error creeping into the estimate due to a portion of exports not being recorded as imports within a given period and a portion of recorded imports being really the exports of a year preceding the period. The excess of total imports over total exports may then be assumed to give an approximate measure of the total amount of freight charges paid by India during the period as a whole. During 1898–99 to 1913–14 the total of India's coastal imports amounted to Rs. 84,536 lakhs, while the value of exports was Rs. 80,140. The excess value of imports which comes to Rs. 4,390 lakhs represents freight and insurance payments by India. This total of freight and insurance bill has got to be distributed over individual years to ascertain India's annual debits on that score. For this we work out the percentage of total freight and insurance charges to the total value of coastal imports and apply it for individual years. Obviously the results are subject to a small margin of error due to the assumption of a constant percentage relation between import values and freight charges every year while in fact this might have been changed because of divergent variations in freight rates and import values. The variations, however, were not so large as to upset rough calculations.

We see, then, that freight and insurance charges together on India's coastal trade amount to 5 per cent of the coastal imports. Professor Findlay Shirras has estimated 15 per cent of the freight and insurance charges as payment for finance, insurance, and other commission charges.[1] By using his estimate we calculate the percentage of pure freight charges to import values as 4·25.

This again is an estimate of the gross earnings of British shipping engaged in India's coastal trade. C. K. Hobson has already calculated that 30 per cent of the gross earnings of British shipping engaged in foreign trade were spent abroad. But this is an average percentage based upon the expenditure of British ships and crew during all sorts of voyages, including long voyages with only temporary halts in foreign ports. Obviously the percentage of expenditure to gross earnings is bound to be higher in the case of ships permanently located abroad and which ply between foreign ports only. The British ships carrying on the coastal trade of India must be spending a large part of their earnings in purchasing provisions and in paying the wages of the crew which is mostly Indian. "In this respect, then, the coasting trade is similar to a firm or an exchange bank doing business in India and what is transferred to England is only the profits of the trade."[2] Unfortunately, however, we have not the slightest information available to ascertain the percentage of these profits to gross earnings. Taking into consideration that the ships engaged in coastal trade stay much longer in Indian harbours than the ships engaged in foreign trade, it can be assumed that about 60 per cent of their earnings are spent in India. This is a purely arbitrary figure and perhaps errs on the conservative side. But on the whole the error resulting from this assumption will form an insignificant percentage of the volume of Indian balance of indebtedness and hence may be ignored.

Professor Findlay Shirras in the paper on "India's Real Balance of Trade in 1922–23," which he read before the seventh

[1] G. F. Shirras, "India's Real Balance of Trade," *Proceedings of the Seventh Indian Economic Conference*, p. 73.

[2] G. F. Shirras, op. cit., p. 77.

TABLE VII

FREIGHT PAYMENTS BY INDIA

(In lakhs of rupees)

Year	*Coastal Imports*	*Freight Charges at 4·25 per cent of the Import Value*	*Net Freight Payments on Coastal Trade**	*Freight Charges on Foreign Trade†*	*Net Freight payments on Foreign Trade‡*	*Total Freight Payments*
1898–99	3,644	155	62	471	330	392
1899–00	4,137	176	70	553	387	457
1900–01	4,830	205	82	567	397	479
1901–02	4,450	189	76	706	494	570
1902–03	4,025	171	68	720	504	572
1903–04	4,268	181	72	695	487	559
1904–05	4,521	192	77	707	495	572
1905–06	5,050	215	86	818	573	659
1906–07	5,705	242	97	542	379	476
1907–08	6,580	280	112	671	470	582
1908–09	5,877	250	100	838	587	687
1909–10	5,670	241	96	680	476	572
1910–11	5,905	251	100	648	454	554
1911–12	6,047	257	103	829	580	683
1912–13	6,702	285	114	1,127	789	903
1913–14	7,125	303	121	1,299	909	1,030

* After allowing 60 per cent of the gross earnings for expenditure in India.
† Supra, Table V.
‡ After allowing 30 per cent of the gross earnings for expenditure in India.

Indian Economic Conference, seems to have unconsciously ignored the debits to India on account of freight and insurance charges on coastal trade. He says: "The expenditure for shipping services and commissions has not been included in the Balance of Trade Statement in the final computation, because under section 30 of the Indian Sea Customs Act the Indian Import Returns include freights and insurance."[1] This reasoning is quite correct so far as our foreign trade is concerned; but it cannot be applied to coastal trade also, which is a branch of the domestic trade. Insurance and freight charges payable by India on her foreign trade appear in the balance of her international transactions along with the imports which are valued c.i.f. The coastal imports, however, are not included in our international transactions and hence freight and insurance charges payable on our coastal trade do not figure in the balance sheet. Therefore these payments should be separately included in the final computation of India's Balance of Trade Statement.

Table VII represents the net amount of freight charges payable by India during 1898–99 to 1913–14.

INSURANCE AND BANKING PAYMENTS, ETC.

Marine Insurance

The earnings of foreign insurance and banking companies constitute an important item in the balance sheet of India's international debits and credits. Most of these companies are branches of British companies registered in Great Britain. In 1882 Sir Robert Giffen calculated the earnings of these concerns at 2·5 per cent of the total of Great Britain's import and export trade. Professor Findlay Shirras after careful inquiries has brought down the estimate for India at 1·5 per cent: 0·5 per cent for insurance charges, 0·25 per cent for banker's commission and bill stamps, and 0·75 per cent for other minor charges.[2] In the absence of any direct information,

[1] G. F. Shirras, op. cit., p. 73. [2] G. F. Shirras, op., cit., p. 78.

we have used this estimate to calculate India's insurance payments on her imports. For coastal trade also Professor Shirras has calculated that 15 per cent of the gross amount of freight and insurance charges constitute insurance and banking payments. Pure insurance payments form one-third of the latter. On this basis the actual percentage of insurance charges to coastal imports works out at 0·25. The earnings of the foreign fire and life insurance companies in India are not taken into account, first, because they cannot be estimated even indirectly and, secondly, because they are insignificant as compared with the total volume of our indebtedness.

PROFITS OF THE EXCHANGE BANKS

"Exchange Banks" is the name applied to foreign banks who have monopolized the financing of India's foreign trade. Almost all of them are branches of larger concerns registered in Great Britain whose operations extend to many other parts of the world. In 1898–99 the number of such banks transacting business in India was eight, which increased to twelve at the end of our period. Of these the Chartered Bank of India, Australia, and China, the National Bank of India, the Mercantile Bank of India, and the Eastern Bank are said to have been doing a considerable part of their business in India.[1] The main items of their business are:

(i) Dealings in foreign exchange.
(ii) Discounting and rediscounting of internal bills.
(iii) Agency Work.

Dealings in foreign exchange are the most important source of profit to the Exchange Banks. Taking out the element of interest from the composite payment they demand from

[1] *Indian Central Banking Enquiry Committee, Majority Report,* p. 310.

importers and exporters there remains a balance which represents charge for the service of changing money from one currency into another. It is suspected that this charge is levied on the whole of our foreign trade and not on the difference between the import and export operations transacted by the banks.[1] In fact, it is only for this difference that they come into the market for more bills or more remittance.

The margin between the deposit rates and the discount rates indicates the profits of the Exchange Banks in discounting internal bills. It is a patent fact that these banks receive deposits in India at lower rates of interest than the Indian Joint-Stock Banks. It is also equally patent that their discount rate is higher than the bank-rate in India. In most other countries it is lower than the bank-rate. The profits earned by the Exchange Banks in discounting internal bills in India may naturally be expected to be considerably high. Moreover, by rediscounting in London at lower rates the export bills discounted in India on the basis of Indian money rates which are higher, they earn an additional handsome commission.

In addition, Exchange Banks make money "by undertaking agency work, purchase of sterling securities by Indians, general remittance work, letters of credit, and rents from bank warehouses. They handle the bulk of what may be called the invisible imports of India, and they make profits out of the movement of permanent capital to India, the withdrawal of capital and the transfer of income on such capital." They are also said to have been earning large profits by managing imports of gold and silver bullion, which was their monopoly for a long time and which even now accounts for a large part of their income. Government remittances even are suspected to be a source of their profits.

Though the profits earned by the Exchange Banks from all

[1] *Indian Central Banking Enquiry Committee, Minority Report*, p. 214.

branches of their business in India are considered to be very high, statistical information on this subject is absolutely lacking. First, there is no way of knowing the amount of capital employed by the Exchange Banks exclusively in India; and secondly, there is no information about the rate of profits earned by them on purely Indian business. Even the Indian Central Banking Enquiry Committee, which reported only recently, could not gather any useful data about the position of these banks in India. Hence to ascertain their approximate earnings resort must be had to a very rough calculation.

As to the proportion of the Foreign Banks' capital employed in this country the Government of India in a letter to the Secretary of State, dated June 13, 1901, wrote: "It is impossible to fix what this proportion may be, but there is reason to believe that considerably less than one-half of the capital of these banks could be made quickly available in India to meet special demands."[1] During 1901 to 1913 four new banks were opened in India. Being new to the field of their operations they cannot be expected to have a large proportion of their total capital with them. We assume that about 25 per cent of the total capital of the Exchange Banks was employed in India during the period of our study. Similarly, the system recently adopted by the Commercial Intelligence Department for the classification of these banks suggests that three of them had a considerable proportion of their business in India. The average of the profits earned by these three banks may therefore be taken as a rough measure of the profits earned by all the banks. But even here the data are incomplete. Information about the rates of dividend declared by only two of the three important banks is available and it also does not cover all the years of our period. The dividend declared by the National Bank of India was 12 per cent per annum for

[1] No. 199, dated June 13, 1901, from the Government of India to the Secretary of State. Quoted in the *Minority Report of the Indian Central Banking Enquiry Committee*, p. 155.

eight years up to 1912 and 16 per cent for 1913, while the dividend declared by the Chartered Bank was 14 per cent for twelve years up to 1918, free of income tax.[1] Thus from 1904 to 1906 we have only the rate of dividend declared by the National Bank of India, and we assume it to represent the rate of profits earned by all the Exchange Banks. From 1910 onwards the rate of profits will be represented by the average of the rates of dividend declared by the National Bank and the Chartered Bank. In the absence of any information relating to the years prior to 1904 the dividend declared by the National Bank in 1904 is assumed to represent the average rate of profits. Accordingly, for all the years up to 1906 the average rate of profits will be 12 per cent, from 1906 to 1912 it will be 13 per cent, and for 1913 it will be 15 per cent.

Payments on account of other minor services in connection with the movement of goods between India and other countries, according to Professor Findlay Shirras, amount to 0·75 per cent of the value of imports. This comes to one-half of all the payments, exclusive of freight charges. On this basis the value of minor services performed by foreign agencies in connection with our coastal trade amounts to 0·37 per cent of the coastal imports.

The estimates of the insurance, banking, and other minor payments by India are presented in Table VIII.

"HOME CHARGES"

"Home charges" represent the expenditure incurred by the Secretary of State for India in England. The main heads of the expenditure are: establishment of the Secretary of State, recruitment of persons for civil and military employment in India and their pensions, purchase of stores and railway construction materials, and interest on India's sterling debt. All this expenditure is borne by India and it constitutes an

[1] *Indian Central Banking Enquiry Committee, Minority Report*, p. 143.

TABLE VIII

Insurance, Banking, and Other Minor Charges

(In lakhs of rupees)

Year	Marine Insurance: I Payments on Coastal Trade*	Marine Insurance: II Payments on Foreign Trade†	Exchange Banks: III Total Capital and Reserve	Exchange Banks: IV Capital and Reserve Employed in India‡	Exchange Banks: V Percentage of Dividend Declared	Exchange Banks: VI Dividend Payable by India	Minor Charges: VII Coastal Trade§	Minor Charges: VIII Foreign Trade‖	Total I + II + VI + VII + VIII
1898–99	9	45	1,314	526	12	63	13	68	198
1899–00	10	48	1,341	536	12	84	15	73	230
1900–01	12	53	1,770	708	12	85	18	80	248
1901–02	11	55	1,753	701	12	84	16	83	249
1902–03	10	56	1,714	686	12	82	15	84	247
1903–04	11	66	2,172	869	12	104	16	94	291
1904–05	11	72	2,230	892	12	107	17	109	316
1905–06	13	77	2,280	912	12	109	19	116	334
1906–07	14	81	2,379	952	13	124	21	122	362
1907–08	16	90	2,500	1,000	13	130	24	135	395
1908–09	15	76	2,503	1,001	13	130	21	115	357
1909–10	14	81	2,842	1,137	13	148	21	122	386
1910–11	15	87	3,259	1,304	13	170	22	131	425
1911–12	15	99	3,390	1,356	13	176	22	149	461
1912–13	17	115	3,547	1,417	13	184	25	173	414
1913–14	18	118	3,546	1,418	15	184	26	177	423

* 0·25 per cent of the value of coastal imports.
† 0·50 per cent of the value of foreign imports.
‡ 25 per cent of the total capital and reserve.
§ 0·37 per cent of the value of coastal imports.
‖ 0·75 per cent of the value of foreign imports.

important debit item in the balance sheet of her international transactions. Here, however, we shall consider the India Office expenses and the charges for the diplomatic services in Persia and China, payments in connection with the Civil Departments in India, payment for the management of the debt, and the Army and Marine effective charges which represent a payment for services rendered to India. Interest charges are discussed elsewhere.

INDIA OFFICE EXPENSES AND THE CHARGES FOR THE DIPLOMATIC SERVICES IN PERSIA AND CHINA

The India Office expenses include the salaries of the Secretary of State for India, Under-Secretaries, members of the India Council, and heads of various departments, and other sundry payments. The charges for diplomatic services in Persia and China were on account of contributions made by India to the expenses of the Mission in Persia and of His Majesty's Establishments in China which were maintained for Imperial purposes. On the recommendation of the Welby Commission, the Indian payment for the diplomatic services in China ceased in 1901 and that for the Persian Mission in 1905. After 1905, therefore, no payment was made by India on this account.

PAYMENTS IN CONNECTION WITH CIVIL DEPARTMENTS IN INDIA

India has annually to pay large subsidies for telegraphic and mail services overseas. Till 1908 she had to pay nearly three lakhs of rupees every year to make good the losses on the Red Sea Telegraph Line constructed in 1858. An alternative telegraph communication between India and England via the Cape and the Mauritius was established in 1890. It is now known as the Zanzibar Mauritius Cable. India had to pay a subsidy of Rs. 150,000 a year on account of this Cable Service. There were also other subsidies payable by India for mail services in the Persian Gulf, for mail services between

India and England and for the telegraphic service controlled by the Indo-European Telegraph Department. All these services are extensions of the Inland Postal and Telegraphic Service and hence payments for them are called as payments in connection with the Civil Departments in India.

PAYMENT FOR THE MANAGEMENT OF THE DEBT

Almost every year the Government of India has to appear in the London Money Market to borrow money. They carry out these loan transactions through the Banks of England and Ireland, who are their London agents and who perform all the necessary services in that connection. It is through these London agents, too, that payment of interest and repayment of loans are made. For this agency work the Banks of England and Ireland receive some remuneration from the Government of India. In the year 1913–14 it amounted to Rs. 9 lakhs.

THE ARMY AND MARINE EFFECTIVE CHARGES

India has annually to remit to the War Office the cost of recruiting and training British soldiers for her. Besides, since the introduction of the "Short-Service" system she has had to contribute to the grant of "Deferred Pay" which is offered as an inducement to British persons to join the Army. The British soldiers in India at the end of their tenure of service—which is ordinarily fixed at five years for the officers and seven years for the privates—are sent back to England and fresh ones are imported. This country had to bear the whole cost of their transportation before 1900. But since then, on the recommendation of the Welby Commission, the British Government has been contributing Rs. 19·5 lakhs towards this cost. The payment of marine effective charges during the period of our study was governed by Lord Rosebery's Award. According to it India had to pay Rs. 15 lakhs to the Admiralty, besides bearing the local expenses of the squadron engaged for the protection of her trade and for general naval defence.

In Table IX figures of net total amount of these payments are reproduced from the *Statistical Abstracts for British India.*

TABLE IX

PAYMENTS ON ACCOUNT OF "HOME CHARGES"*

(In lakhs of rupees)

Year	*India Office Expenses etc.*†	*Payments in Connection with Civil Departments in India*	*Payment for the Management of "Debt"*	*Net Army and Marine Effective Charges*‡	*Total*
1898–99	24	19	7	183	233
1899–00	24	24	6	163	217
1900–01	25	21	7	153	206
1901–02	27	25	6	29	87
1902–03	36	30	6	159	231
1903–04	36	25	6	117	184
1904–05	34	27	6	104	171
1905–06	36	24	6	78	144
1906–07	31	27	7	107	172
1907–08	34	24	7	118	183
1908–09	36	19	9	162	226
1909–10	33	18	9	144	204
1910–11	33	21	10	158	222
1911–12	42	22	9	145	218
1912–13	33	22	9	153	217
1913–14	36	25	9	150	220

* Compiled from the *Statistical Abstracts for British India.*
† Include India's contribution for His Majesty's Establishments in China till the year 1901, and for the Persian Mission till 1905.
‡ After deducting military receipts in England.

TOURISTS' EXPENDITURE, ETC.

The money spent by foreign tourists in India forms a credit item in her international transactions, while a similar expenditure by Indian travellers abroad constitutes a debit item. About the expenditure of foreign tourists in India no information whatsoever is available for the period of our study. On the other hand, the expenditure of Indian students reading in foreign universities, who formed the most numerous class of Indian visitors to Europe and other countries, amounted to about 30 lakhs of rupees a year.[1] The remittances to foreign travellers in India and to Indian students abroad are, however, made either through the Post Office or through the Exchange Banks whose transactions we have considered elsewhere.

TABLE X

BALANCE OF PAYMENTS FOR SERVICES EXCEPT INTEREST CHARGES

(*In lakhs of rupees*)

Year	*Freight Payments by India**	*Insurance, Banking and other Minor Charges†*	*Home Charges‡*	*Total (Debit)*
1898–99	392	198	233	823
1899–00	457	230	217	904
1900–01	479	248	206	933
1901–02	570	249	87	906
1902–03	572	247	231	1,050
1903–04	559	291	184	1,034
1904–05	572	316	171	1,059
1905–06	659	334	144	1,137
1906–07	476	362	172	1,010
1907–08	582	395	183	1,160
1908–09	687	357	226	1,270
1909–10	572	386	204	1,162
1910–11	554	425	222	1,201
1911–12	683	461	218	1,362
1912–13	903	414	217	1,534
1913–14	1,030	423	220	1,673

* Supra, Table VII. † Supra, Table VIII.
‡ Supra, Table IX, does not include interest charges.

Therefore, inasmuch as the expenditures of foreign tourists in India and of Indian students abroad were met by these remittances they have already been accounted for.

The net debits to India on account of the import of services excepting the services of capital are given in Table X.

[1] T. Morrison, *The Economic Transition in India*, p. 192.

CHAPTER III

BALANCE OF NON-COMMERCIAL TRANSACTIONS

NON-COMMERCIAL transactions are a part of the "invisible" items figuring in the balance sheet of a country. Tributes or indemnities, pensions and allowances payable abroad, charities, settlers' effects, immigrants' and emigrants' remittances, and the capital taken out by them at the time of departure are a few of the items coming under this category. They are non-commercial in the sense that the movement of goods on their account is one-sided in character, requiring no off-setting payment in the opposite direction. However, like all other transactions they do affect the balance of international credits and debits. The French indemnity of 1873, the remittances of immigrants[1] in America during the pre-war times, and the post-war flood of American charities[2] to Europe were in their time sufficiently large to upset the trade balances of the countries concerned. In recent years the payment of reparations has been the greatest factor affecting the trade of Germany.

Non-commercial remittances by aliens in India are made either through Money Orders and British Postal Orders or by means of other financial documents. Naturally, provision must be made in foreign countries for the cashing of these documents in either of the two ways or by both: by exporting additional goods and/or by reducing the imports. Therefore, non-commercial transactions which involve payments by Indians to persons abroad affect the commodity balance of the trade of India, either by increasing the exports or by reducing the imports or in both ways simultaneously. In any case, they

[1] C. F. Speare estimates $250,000,000 as the amount remitted by the foreign immigrants in United States of America during the year 1907. *North American Review*, January 1908, p. 109.

[2] F. W. Taussig, *International Trade*, p. 322.

bring about an excess of exports. Similarly, non-commercial transactions involving payments to India from foreign countries increase the imports or decrease the exports and thus bring about an excess of imports over exports. Settlers' effects, however, which move with their owners without money being used at any stage, in no way affect the balance of international credits and debits. We have already made allowance for this factor in dealing with the commodity balance of trade. Therefore the items which we have to evaluate in striking the balance of non-commercial transactions for India are: first, monetary capital brought in by immigrants and taken out by emigrants; second, remittances by aliens in India to their relatives in the Home Country and by Indians abroad to their relatives at home, remittances by Indians to their relations abroad and conversely by aliens to their people here, and, third, remittances of pensions and allowances payable abroad.

IMMIGRANTS' CAPITAL

Statistical information about immigration to India is extremely scanty, it is non-existent so far as emigration is concerned. However, some details about the movement of coolies from India to various colonies and back are available, and it is possible to form a rough estimate of the capital brought in by coolie immigrants.

The "colonial emigration"[1] from India during the period of our study was controlled by legislation. It was based on what is known as the "indenture" system. According to this system the emigrating Indian labourer in consideration for a wage and the cost of his passage undertook to leave India

[1] Under the Emigration Act XXI of 1883 an Indian emigrant is one who goes by sea under contract to labour for hire to some country other than Ceylon and the Straits Settlements. These countries are excepted on account of their proximity and of the similarity of their general conditions to those of India. The emigration under this Act is in other terms styled "Colonial Emigrations." *Moral and Material Progress Report, 1890–91*, p. 209.

and serve his master in a distant colony for a fixed period which varied from one month to five years. On the termination of his contract he had the option to renew the contract or to settle in the colony and work as he pleased, or to return to his motherland at the expense of the colony which imported him.[1] In this fashion the employer could secure a sufficient supply of labour for a maximum period at a minimum cost. The labourer who agreed to the terms of the contract was generally very poor, having no resources in India even for bare maintenance. From the time of his recruitment all his expenses were borne by the importing colony,[2] where on landing he was entitled to receive a regular wage. Under these circumstances it is difficult to suppose that the labourers emigrating from India to colonies according to the indenture system carried any substantial amount of monetary capital with them.

In the case of immigrants the situation was altogether different. They were the emigrant labourers who had stayed in a colony for some years and earned regular wages. Moreover, as we have said before, the emigrants at the expiration of their agreement were free to take up other employments. Many of them settled in the colonies permanently, acquired land or engaged in retail trading and miscellaneous occupations.[3]

[1] National Bureau of Economic Research, *International Migrations*, vol. ii, p. 597.

[2] *Moral and Material Progress Report*, *1901–2*, p. 320.

[3] *Census of India*, *1911*, p. 97. In Natal there has been a great deal of permanent settlement, and of the total number of Indians enumerated there nearly half were born in the colony. Many of these have forgotten their native language and now talk only English. But it is in Mauritius that the process of colonization has made most headway. The introduction of Indian coolies to work the sugar plantations dates from the emancipation of the slaves, three-quarters of a century ago, and from that time onwards many of the coolies who have gone there have made the island their permanent home. Though it now contains only 35,000 persons who were born in India, the total number of Indians is 258,000, or about 70 per cent of the whole population. A large part of the land is now owned by Indians and they are dominant in commercial, agricultural, and domestic callings.

Available evidence goes to prove that those who stayed on in this manner prospered and did much better in life than they could have done by returning to India. The figures in Table XI show the total resident Indian population indentured and free in the chief labour-importing colonies, and their savings per head during the years 1900–1 and 1910–11.

TABLE XI*

RESIDENT INDIAN EMIGRANTS IN THE CHIEF LABOUR IMPORTING COLONIES AND THEIR SAVINGS PER HEAD

Colony	*Indian Population in 1900–01*	*Savings per Head in 1900–01* Rs. as. ps.	*Indian Population in 1910–11*	*Savings per Head in 1910–11* Rs. as. ps.
British Guiana..	—	—	1,32,984	33 6 0
Trinidad ..	85,615	17 12 0	1,07,433	17 14 0
Mauritius ..	2,65,163	13 4 0	2,59,975	89 0 0
Natal	65,925	23 3 0	1,08,694	16 6 0
Fiji	15,368	19 13 0	39,314	6 3 0
Jamaica ..	15,278	23 14 0	15,415	80 4 0
Surinam ..	18,000	26 3 0	27,358	19 5 0
Demerara ..	1,25,875	21 10 0	—	—
St. Lucia ..	1,200	23 13 0	—	—
Martinique ..	3,764	0 8 0	—	—
Guadeloupe ..	15,276	2 12 0	—	—
Total ..	6,11,464		6,91,173	

* Compiled from the *Moral and Material Progress Reports*, 1901–2 and 1911–12.

The figures of savings are necessarily incomplete and they are not all comparable with one another. In all cases they include bank deposits and amounts remitted by emigrants to India, but the Fiji figures for savings banks represent only deposits made during the year, while in other cases the total amount held in deposit in the banks is shown. For the year 1900–1 the value of landed and other property in the possession of emigrants is also included in the figures of savings per head, while for the year 1910–11 it is included only in the figures for British Guiana, Mauritius, Jamaica, and Surinam. The residents of British Guiana, Mauritius, Natal, Jamaica, and Surinam seem to have been better off than others. Natives of India and their descendants constituted 70 per cent of the total population of Mauritius in 1910–11 and owned landed property to the estimated value of Rs. 18,000,000.[1] In regard to remittances made to India by money orders the emigrant population of Natal easily stands first. The amount remitted from that colony in the year 1911 was about Rs. 1,050,000, or on an average Rs. 9–6–0 for every resident Indian. Remittances from Fiji averaged about Rs. 1–3–0, while in the case of other colonies the average was less than 12 annas per head.

These residents, when they returned to India, could naturally be expected to have brought an appreciable amount of monetary capital. Even the regular wage-earners who turned back to the Mother Country soon after the expiration of their contracts, which extended from five years to ten years, may be credited with large savings. Figures for the monetary capital brought in by the immigrant coolies landing at Calcutta can be gleaned from the *Moral and Material Progress* reports. From these data we work out the per capita amount of monetary capital brought in by the coolies arriving at Calcutta and apply their average to the rest of their kind. There cannot be any serious objection to this procedure. First, because since the year 1904–5 the coolie emigrants landing at Calcutta formed a large percentage of total coolie emigrants returning to India. Secondly, the emigrant labourers landing at Calcutta, Bombay, or Madras did not come from any one colony but from all the colonies, and hence the average *per capita* amount of monetary capital brought in by the emigrants at any of these ports will be largely representative of the rest. The estimates prepared on this basis for the whole period under study are presented in Table XII.

The figures for monetary capital brought into India as far as

[1] *Moral and Material Progress Report, 1911–12*, p. 374.

they go may be approximately correct. But colonial immigration is only a fraction of total immigration into India from the outside world. Similarly with emigration. Again, no data about the total annual volume of immigration and emigration

TABLE XII*

CAPITAL BROUGHT IN BY THE COOLIE IMMIGRANTS

Year	*Coolie Immigrants*†	*Per Capita Amount of Capital Brought in*‡	*Total Capital Brought in by the Coolie Immigrants*
		Rs.	*Rs.*
1898–99	5,689	129	7,33,983
1899–00	9,484	159	15,08,061
1900–01	7,006	139	9,62,992
1901–02	10,623	210	22,65,830
1902–03	12,757	183	23,04,123
1903–04	11,673	167	19,48,264
1904–05	6,341	174	11,05,851
1905–06	6,945	173	11,96,006
1906–07	8,197	160	13,08,910
1907–08	6,774	177	12,03,474
1908–09	7,918	180	14,19,780
1909–10	6,909	171	11,82,528
1910–11	5,788	154	8,91,394
1911–12		155	
1912–13	4,641	197	12,15,047
1913–14	5,284	180	9,55,440

* Compiled from the *Moral and Material Progress Reports.*

† All the immigrants did not bring savings to India.

‡ See Appendix II for the *per capita* savings brought by immigrants from different colonies. In calculating the *per capita* brought in by these immigrants no account has been taken of those immigrants who did not bring in any savings.

are available. The census reports record the number of immigrants arriving in India during the census years, but say nothing about emigration. The data are so scanty that even indirect methods cannot be used to ascertain the inflow and outflow of population every year. Still, in general terms it can be said that a majority of immigrants into India come from Asiatic countries, especially from across the Nepal Frontier. Of the Nepalese enumerated in India in the year 1911 a considerable number were sepoys in the Army, and in military police battalions, and their dependants. Many of them were engaged in breeding buffaloes, making ghee, or working as sawyers in the Government forests of Assam.[1] Most of the Chinese immigrants, whose number is swelling every year, are found in Burma,

TABLE XIII

IMMIGRANTS FROM OUTSIDE INDIA AT THE CENSUS YEARS 1891, 1901, AND 1911

	Immigrants from			
	I	II	III	IV
Year	*Contiguous Countries*	*Other Asiatic Countries*	*United Kingdom*	*Other European Countries*
1891	4,60,616	60,988	97,921	7,148
1901	3,65,441	160,708	96,653	7,930
1911	3,80,135	124,978	122,919	9,049

	Immigrants from			
	V	VI	VII	VIII
Year	*America*	*Africa*	*Australia*	*Total*
1891	2,325	11,565	503	6,41,066
1901	2,069	8,293	646	6,41,740
1911	2,760	10,270	1,267	6,51,378

where they are in demand as shoe-makers and carpenters. Immigrants from Europe and America find remunerative jobs ready for them in India. In the year 1911 the total number of immigrants recorded from outside Asia was 146,265. Of these 131,968 came from Europe, the United Kingdom alone claiming 122,919. Of the British-born, 77,626 were serving in the Army and the rest were absorbed by railways and industrial concerns.[2] The number of immigrants in India at the three census years 1891, 1901, and 1911 is represented in Table XIII according to the country of immigration.

[1] *Census of India, Report, 1911*, vol. i, p. 96. [2] Ibid., p. 97.

A cursory glance at these figures brings two important facts to our notice. In the first place immigrants from the United Kingdom during the decade 1901 to 1911 showed a large increase and, secondly, the figure for total immigrants was more or less constant for all the three years. These data, however, are extremely scrappy to form the basis of an estimate of the annual flow of immigration. So far as the volume of emigration is concerned even guesswork is not possible. Moreover, we could not find any reference anywhere to the probable amount of monetary capital brought in and taken out by immigrants and emigrants respectively. Obviously in the absence of such fundamental data it is impossible to calculate even approximately the amounts of monetary capital brought in and taken out by immigrants and emigrants respectively. But on general grounds it can be stated that as most of the immigrants come to India in search of employment, and as most of the emigrants are immigrants returning to their home countries after a period of highly remunerative service in India, the net balance on account of the movements of monetary capital accompanying the migrants in either direction will be a debit item. This is especially the case with European immigration and emigration, which is most important to India so far as the transfer of monetary capital is concerned.

MEANS OF REMITTANCE FROM INDIA

Even though we have not been able to ascertain separately the net debit or credit balance on account of the monetary capital brought in and taken out by immigrants and emigrants, it is possible to calculate approximately the balance of non-commercial transactions as a whole. The transfer of money from one country to another, whether it be the capital of a departing immigrant or emigrant or the remittance by a resident of one country to his friends or relatives in the other, as effected either through a bank or by a money order. In the case of India there is a third way of sending money and that is by the purchase of British postal orders. Remittances of pensions and allowances payable abroad are effected by means of Council Bills. The illiterate or otherwise ignorant immigrants from the contiguous Asiatic countries and the Indian emigrants to the colonies for the most part make use of the facilities afforded by the Post Office. Foreign money orders to and from the United Kingdom, most of the British colonies and possessions, foreign European countries, and most of their colonies and possessions, and Egypt are issued in sterling, payments being made by the remitters and to the payees in India at the rates of exchange fixed by the Post Office from time to time for this purpose.[1] On the other hand, European immigrants and their relatives at home effect remittances through the British Exchange Banks and other foreign banks having branches in India. Remittances to Indian students studying in the United Kingdom are also generally made in this fashion. If we take account of all the media of transfer issued and paid in India by these agencies the resultant will closely represent the net balance of non-commercial transactions for India.

FOREIGN MONEY-ORDER TRANSACTIONS

There are available for India statistics of postal money orders issued in India and payable in other countries. All these money orders, however, do not represent non-commercial remittances from India. About 50 per cent of the amount goes to cover small business transactions. This figure is based on the value of articles imported by post in the year 1898–99 as a percentage of the total amount of postal money orders issued in India and payable abroad during the same year. The actual percentage works out a little higher.[2] But we have made some

[1] *Annual Report of the Posts and Telegraphs, 1893–94*, p. 17.

[2] In 1898–99 the value of articles imported by post was Rs. 33,42,000, while the value of foreign orders issued and British

allowance for the transactions settled through the Exchange Banks which were just beginning to make headway. We further assume that this percentage remained more or less constant during the period 1898–99 to 1913–14. Admittedly these assumptions rest on a somewhat slender basis:

(i) In the first place the value of foreign money orders issued in India increased at a very slow rate during the period of our study.[1]

(ii) Secondly, the number of European immigrants in India increased by over 30,000 during the decade 1901 to 1911.

(iii) Thirdly, the value of articles imported by post also increased fast, so much so that it over-balanced the value of foreign money orders issued and British Postal Orders purchased every year since 1905.[2]

(iv) Lastly, the business of the Exchange Banks in regard to private remittances showed a remarkable progress during the period.

The slow rise in the value of foreign money orders issued in India, in spite of an addition of 30,000 to the number of European immigrants residing in India, to whom a large share of the total remittances from India is usually credited, indicates that the Post Office did not find favour with them as an agency for the transfer of money. On the other hand, the progressive remittance business of the Exchange Banks simultaneously with the increase of European immigrants and the overwhelming increase in the total value of articles imported by post suggests that the remittances by the immigrants and

postal orders purchased was Rs. 49,00,000. Therefore the actual percentage of commercial remittances to the total value of foreign money orders issued to British postal orders purchased in India comes to sixty-seven.

[1] Vide Table XIV.

[2] *Review of the Trade of India, 1931–32.*

the payments for the articles imported by post were made through the Exchange Banks. Moreover, as we have already stated, the postal money orders were a favourite means of remittance with the illiterate and ignorant immigrants who did not know the technicalities of the procedure of the Exchange Banks. The earnings of this class were not very large and hence the value of foreign money orders issued in India did not show any substantial increase.

BRITISH POSTAL ORDERS

Money can also be transferred to countries outside India by means of British postal orders. These orders are sold in India at the Post Office for a small commission and can be remitted to the United Kingdom and other British colonies where alone they are payable. However, they were not very popular with the people during the period of our study, nor were they entirely non-commercial in nature. The percentage of the value of commercial foreign money orders to the value of total foreign money orders issued in India may be applied here also. In addition, since October 1, 1905, these orders were made payable in India, and like inland money orders were used for local remittances.[1] Therefore the value of such orders paid in India, along with those remitted to settle commercial transactions, must be deducted from the total value of orders sold in India to arrive at the value of non-commercial remittances effected through them. All the necessary information on this account is available in the *Annual Report of the Posts and Telegraphs*.

Just as in the case of foreign money orders issued in India and British postal orders purchased a percentage of their value has been attributed to commercial transactions already accounted for in the commodity balance of trade, similarly some allowance must be made for commercial remittances in the case of foreign money orders payable in India. Here

[1] *Annual Report of the Posts and Telegraphs, 1905–6*, p. 18.

the allowance will be based on the actual percentage which the value of articles exported from India by post bore to the total value of foreign money orders payable in India. First, because the values of individual parcels exported by post were small enough to be paid by money orders and, secondly, their total value was always smaller than the value of foreign money orders payable in India. In the case of foreign money orders issued in India and articles imported by post both these conditions were exactly opposite.[1] The value of commercial money orders calculated in this manner amounted approximately to 30 per cent of the total value of foreign money orders payable in India,[2] which will have to be subtracted from the latter in calculating the balance of non-commercial transactions.

THROUGH FOREIGN MONEY ORDERS

Lastly, before arriving at the final balance of non-commercial money-order transactions we have to deal with the value of "through foreign money orders." "Through foreign money orders" are defined as money orders issued by one foreign

[1] Jewellery, precious stones, gold and silver thread, cigarettes and cinematograph films are the most important articles imported in India by post. The large amounts payable by India on account of these articles can be judged from the value of diamonds alone imported by post for the following years:

		Rs.
1920–21	=	14,60,000
1921–22	=	15,00,000
1922–23	=	132,00,000

League of Nations' *Memorandum on Balance of Payments and Foreign Trade Balances, 1910–23*, vol. ii, p. 319.

[2]

Year	*Foreign Money Orders Payable in India* I	*Articles Exported by Post* II	*Percentage of* II *to* I *Approximate*
	lakhs	*lakhs*	
1898	89	27	30
1908	192	48	30
1913	374	112	30

country for payment in another foreign country, the payment being made through India as an intermediary.[1] When these money orders are received by India from the foreign country of issue they are regarded as equivalent to inward foreign money orders. The credits to India on this account are the amount of the money orders plus a half per cent commission, and are put under the heading of foreign money orders paid. When the sums are sent by India to foreign countries of payment, they are regarded as equivalent to outward foreign money orders. The debits against India on this account are the amounts of the money orders minus a commission. The sums are put under the heading of foreign money orders issued.

From the definition of "through foreign money orders" and the manner in which their accounts are recorded, it follows that the difference between the sums credited and debited to India on account of "through foreign money orders" should be equal to the one-half per cent commission on the inward "through foreign money orders," plus a varying commission on the outward "through foreign money orders."[2] In fact, however, the difference between the two as calculated from the *Statistical Abstract for British India* (Postal Tables) and the Annual Postal Reports is much larger than can possibly be explained on this hypothesis.[3] For instance, the value of

[1] *Posts and Telegraphs Manual*, vol. 6, Appendix C, p. 517.

[2] Ibid., p. 579.

[3] The difference is calculated as follows:

Neither the Statistical Abstracts nor the Postal Reports give separate figures for through foreign money orders. The Postal Reports even do not mention the term. The Statistical Abstracts from 1921–22 to date, however, refer to them indirectly. The figures for foreign money orders paid and issued given in the Abstracts are—reference to footnotes—taken to exclude through foreign money orders. Hence up to 1920–21 the figures given in the Statistical Abstracts and in the Annual Postal Reports tally. But from 1921–22 they too differ. Therefore, if on the basis of this evidence as well as of an absence of indications to the contrary, we assume that the figures in the "through foreign money orders" issued by India during the year 1921–22 was Rs. 4,22,172, while that of the "through foreign money orders" paid to India was Rs. 7,52,153. The difference of Rs. 3,29,981 obviously cannot be explained as due to commission charges, which form only a very small percentage of the total value of "through foreign money orders" issued and paid in India.[1] We have not as yet been able to find any explanation of this discrepancy between the recorded statistics and our theoretic calculations, which are apparently based on correct principles. However, since the figures of "through foreign money orders" involved in our calculations are insignificant relatively to the total trade of India we have thought it proper to ignore them.

Table XIV represents the balance of non-commercial remittances effected by means of foreign money orders and British postal orders.

REMITTANCES THROUGH EXCHANGE BANKS

As said before, remittances are also made through banks. Naturally their value will be included in this account only so far as they relate to non-commercial transactions. But infor-

Annual Postal Reports include those for all types of foreign money orders—including through foreign money orders—then for the years 1921–22 onward the difference between the figures in the Postal Reports and the Statistical Abstracts should be a measure of the amounts of through foreign money orders.

[1] The wide gap between the sums credited and debited to India on account of "through foreign money orders" can be seen from the following figures:

	Values in lakhs of rupees	
Year	*Credits*	*Debits*
1921–22	7	4
1922–23	3	3
1923–24	3	3
1924–25	2	8
1925–26	3	8
1926–27	5	18
1927–28	9	17

TABLE XIVIII*

Balance of Non-Commercial Remittances Effected by Means of Foreign Money Orders and British Postal Orders

(*In lakhs of rupees*)

	Debits			Credits		
	I	II	III	IV	V	
Year	*Foreign Money Orders Issued in India*	*Net British Postal Orders Payable Abroad*	*Total of I and II After Allowing 50 % for Commercial remittances*†	*Foreign Money Orders Payable in India*‡	IV *After Allowing 30 % for Commercial Remittances*†	*Balance of Non-Commercial Remittances* V–III (*Credit*)
1898–99	43	6	25	89	62	37
1899–00	43	6	25	105	73	48
1900–01	46	8	27	129	90	63
1901–02	58	10	34	143	100	66
1902–03	59	12	36	149	104	68
1903–04	61	14	38	166	116	78
1904–05	66	16	41	179	125	84
1905–06	71	18	45	192	134	89
1906–07	74	19	47	221	155	108
1907–08	78	23	51	246	172	121
1908–09	88	27	58	210	147	89
1909–10	84	28	56	225	157	101
1910–11	81	27	54	279	195	141
1911–12	80	26	53	301	211	158
1912–13	81	26	54	344	241	187
1913–14	83	27	55	374	262	207

* Compiled from the *Annual Report of Posts and Telegraphs.*

† In so far as the recorded figures of foreign money orders issued and paid in India include the figures for through foreign money orders the results of these columns are a little exaggerated. The error, however, is negligible for our purpose.

‡ See Appendix II for *per capita* remittances made by Indian emigrants residing in various colonies.

TABLE XV

TOTAL BALANCE OF NON-COMMERCIAL TRANSACTIONS

(In lakhs of rupees)

Year	*Net Balance on Account of Remittances through Foreign Money Orders and British Postal Orders** *(credit)*	*Net Balance of Remittances Made Through Banks†* *(Debit)*	*Net Balance of Remittances Made Through Council Bills‡* *(Debit)*	*Final Balance of Non-Commercial Transactions* *(Debit)*
1898–99	37	210	731	904
1899–00	48	210	746	908
1900–01	63	210	714	861
1901–02	66	210	724	868
1902–03	68	210	733	875
1903–04	78	210	739	871
1904–05	84	210	745	871
1905–06	89	210	741	862
1906–07	108	210	758	860
1907–08	121	210	785	874
1908–09	89	210	791	912
1909–10	101	210	798	907
1910–11	141	225	504	588
1911–12	158	240	805	887
1912–13	187	255	831	899
1913–14	207	270	834	897

* Supra, Table XIV.
† *Report of the Controller of Currency, 1913–14*, p. 52.
‡ *Statistical Abstracts Relating to British India.*

mation about such remittances is extremely scanty to enable us to form any independent estimate. Mr. H. F. Howard, formerly the Controller of Currency in India, has, however, prepared a rough estimate of the debits to India on this account.[1] According to one of the Exchange Banks the net debit balance to India on account of non-commercial remittances to and from India made through banks is about Rs. 15,00,000–Rs. 18,00,000 per mensem. Howard assumes the smaller amount at the beginning of the period of our study and gradually increases it to the higher of these figures at the end. In the absence of any other estimate or the necessary data we assume these figures to be approximately correct and adopt them in our study.

Information about remittances of pensions and allowances has been taken from the *Statistical Abstracts for British India.*

The total balance of non-commercial remittances effected through banks and by means of foreign money orders and British postal orders is presented in Table XV.

[1] *Report on the Operations of the Currency Department, the Movement of Funds, and on the Resource Operations of the Government of India for the year 1913–14*, Appendix I, p. 53.

CHAPTER IV

INDIA'S BALANCE OF INDEBTEDNESS

THE difference between all the credit and debit obligations of India, immediate as well as deferred, represents her balance of indebtedness. It is equivalent to the difference between her foreign borrowings and foreign loans. So far we have taken into account India's international credits and debits on account of commodity transactions, service transactions excepting interest payments and non-commercial transactions. But there are certain items which could not be appropriately included under either of these categories and which, accordingly, have escaped reckoning. To ascertain the balance of indebtedness which represents the difference between all the credits and all the debits, those items in our international balance sheet which have escaped computation so far will be considered here in the following order:

Councils and Reverse Councils.
Cash Balances and Reserves of the Secretary of State.
Railway Annuities and Sinking Fund.
India Bills.
Movement of Securities.
Miscellaneous Deposits and Remittances.
Interest Payments.

COUNCILS AND REVERSE COUNCILS

Councils, or the Council Bills as they were properly termed, were the bills drawn by the Secretary of State on India. They were sold in London for sterling and are generally cashed at the Indian treasuries in rupees. In certain cases, when they were specifically drawn either against the Paper Currency Reserve or the Gold Standard Reserve, they were paid from the portions of these reserves kept in India. Reverse Councils, on the other hand, were bills drawn on the Secretary of State for India and payable in London in sterling.

Normally, the commodity balance of trade is favourable to India. Every year she has to receive payments from abroad for the surplus of her exports over imports. On the contrary, the Secretary of State for India has to make payments in London on account of Home Charges. These payments are to be made in sterling while the Indian Revenue to which they are charged is collected in rupees. Therefore, taking advantage of the normally favourable commodity balance of trade and the consequent demand for bills on India, the Secretary of State sold "Councils" and got command over funds in London to meet his liabilities. The bills were offered in London for tender at the Bank of England every Wednesday morning and there was a reserve price below which no tender was accepted. The purchasers remitted the bills to India, where on presentation to the Treasury they were cashed out of the accumulated surplus of rupees, and the claims of the Indian exporters were satisfied. Whenever the Indian bank-rate was high, the Secretary of State for India sold "Telegraphic Transfers" instead of Council Bills. By means of these Telegraphic Transfers rupees could be obtained in India almost as soon as the sovereigns were paid into the Secretary of State's account at the Bank of England. In effect, therefore, the "Council Bills" and the "Telegraphic Transfers" were the means of transferring funds from India to London and vice versa, which saved the Government of India the extra expenditure on the export of gold to London, so as to purchase the amount of sterling necessary to honour their debit obligations in Great Britain. They also brought a small commission to the Secretary of State for India for dealing in foreign exchange, which otherwise would have been secured by the London banks.

Till the year 1900 the volume of "Council Bills" drawn by the Secretary of State was mainly governed by the amount required to defray the Home Charges. Since 1900, however, the functions of the Council Bill system were enlarged and for the rest of the period of our study it played a very important part in the maintenance of the Gold Exchange Standard.[1] Sales of Council Bills during this period were determined by the necessity of maintaining the 1s. 4d. ratio.

How are these Council Bills to be accounted in the balance sheet of India's international transactions? Are they to be considered as debits because they represent a payment for the surplus of our exports, or are they to be considered as credits because they represent a transfer of funds from India to London? As we have already said, Council Bills are only a means of transmitting funds. However, they perform a double transaction. When the Councils are sold by the Secretary of State the proceeds of the sale represent credits to India. But when the bills are cashed through the Treasury in India they become a debit item. If, therefore, the Council Bills are to be included in the balance of India's international transactions they may be considered both as credits and debits or they may be excluded altogether. The following passage from the Report of the Controller of Currency, 1913–14, is enlightening on this point:

> The remittances which the Indian Government have to make to England to meet their liabilities in the United Kingdom on account of interest and other charges are usually effected by the sale by the Secretary of State of bills and telegraphic transfers on India. These bills, etc., represent two transactions, namely, a remittance to England by the Government of India and a corresponding remittance to India by the purchaser of bills. The relationship between these remittances and the other private transactions can be represented in the form of a simple equation:
>
> $$C = D + S,$$
>
> where C represents the private credits on account of exports, etc.,

[1] J. M. Keynes, *Indian Currency and Finance*, p. 106.

D the debits including imports, etc., and S the Secretary of State's drawings by which payment is made for the balance of credits not set off by the imports of merchandise, specie, etc. In a similar equation to show the Government transactions, S representing an export of funds from their point of view may appear on the other side of the account and we should have

$$C + S = D$$

where C represents credits and D the debits on account of Government. The two equations can obviously be combined into one, thus:

$$C + c + S = D + d + S$$

or eliminating S,

$$C + c = D + d.$$

That is to say, the Government and private transactions can be presented in a single equation, and the Secretary of State's drawings, which when this is done represent merely a book transaction, can be eliminated from the joint account.

The Reverse Councils are sold in India and are payable in sterling in London. This process, which is the opposite of that involved by the Council Bills, gives them their name. However, in their effect on the balance of our international transactions they are on a par with the Council Bills.

CASH BALANCES AND RESERVES OF THE SECRETARY OF STATE

The discussion about the real nature of transactions effected by means of the Council Bills leads us to the consideration of the credits and debits of India managed by the Secretary of State. His balance sheet in any year includes:[1]

Receipts

(i) Net debt incurred.
(ii) Council Bills.
(iii) Gold Remittances from India.
(iv) Other miscellaneous deposits and remittances.
(v) Opening Balance.

[1] See footnote on next page.

Disbursements

(i) Net Home Charges payable.
(ii) Capital expenditure in England.
(iii) Reverse Councils.
(iv) Purchase of silver.
(v) Closing balance.

The Council Bills and the Reverse Councils we are altogether omitting from the balance of India's international transactions because they represent two opposite transactions. The rest of the credit and debit items enumerated above, except the withdrawals and additions to the Treasury and other reserves of the Secretary of State, are considered elsewhere in the course of this study. Now, therefore, the point is whether these withdrawals and additions to the balances of the Secretary of State be included or not in the balance sheet of India's international transactions, and if they are to be

NOTE TO PAGE 87.—J. M. Keynes arranges the balance sheet of the Secretary of State as follows:

PAYMENTS

Home charges	x
Gold "Earmarked," or securities bought for Currency Reserve in London	y
Cost of silver—profit on coinage credited to Gold Standard Reserve in London	z
Expenditure on stores in London for capital purposes in India	v
Transfer of cash balances from India to London . . .	$\pm w$

Total payments $= x - y - z - v \pm w$.

RECEIPTS

Council Bills cashed from balances in India	$x - u - v \pm w$
Council Bills cashed from rupees in Currency Reserve in India	y
Council Bills cashed from new coinage .	z
Total Council Bills drawn	$x - y - z - u - v \pm w$
Net Capital Borrowings	u

Total Receipts in London $= x + y + z + v \pm w$

included what is their significance. In taking account of India's international credits we have considered all the remittances from India to the Secretary of State on Government account as credits. However, such remittances, whether made in gold or by means of the Secretary of State's drawings, have *per se* no more effect on the international transactions of India than the transfer of funds from one Treasury in India to another. "What is material is the extent to which they have been actually employed in meeting debits raised against the Government of India in England, and how far any portion of them is still in hand."[1] Accordingly, the part of the remittances which remains after all the debits in England are paid for and which consequently swells the reserves and the cash balances of the Secretary of State cannot be considered as a credit to India. Therefore the inclusion of the entire amount of Government remittances under "credits" has unduly increased their volume to the extent that they added to the reserves and the cash balances of the Government in England. As a set-off against this over-estimate the annual net increase in the reserves and the cash balances of the Secretary of State will be considered as a debit to India. On the other hand, when the remittances of the Government and the loans raised in England are not sufficient to pay off the debits of the Secretary of State, he has to draw upon his reserves and the cash balances. Naturally, to the extent that he draws upon these reserves his credits increase. These credits, however, are so far left unaccounted for, with the result that the total of our receipts on international account represents an under-estimate. It can be corrected by adding the amount of annual net withdrawals from the Secretary of State's reserves and cash balances to the credit side of India's international transactions.

The credits and debits to India on account of alterations in the Secretary of State's reserves and cash balances are presented in Table XVI.

[1] *Report on the Operations of the Currency Department, 1913–14*, p. 50.

international indebtedness is affected in reverse directions in the years of flotation and redemption or funding respectively. Therefore in the year of flotation such loans are considered as credits to India and in the year of redemption or funding they are considered as debits. Though the India Bills issued and redeemed by the Secretary of State represent movements of capital to and from India because they are very small and because their effect on India's balance of indebtedness is cancelled within a very short period of time, they are considered here separately from the larger movements of capital considered elsewhere.

MOVEMENT OF SECURITIES

In their effect on the balance of India's credits and debits the private remittances of securities must be differentiated from the remittances of money.[1] The money remitted from India constitutes a debit item. But if somebody in India sells an Indian security to a person residing in a foreign country the transaction counts in the international trade as a means of discharging an international liability. On the other hand, the remittances of such securities to India from abroad create a liability against her. This is equally true in the case of Indian Government paper enfaced in India for payment of interest in England and vice versa, subject to the qualification that if an Englishman in India saves money and invests it in such paper, and when returning to England gets the paper enfaced and takes it with him, the transaction does not affect the international account of the year one way or the other. Subsequently, however, when interest on such paper falls due a debit arises against India. The net credits and debits on account of the movement of Government securities are therefore included in striking the balance of India's international obligations.

[1] H. F. Howard, op. cit., p. 83.

MISCELLANEOUS DEPOSITS AND REMITTANCES

These include the unrecorded exports on Government account and a number of adjustments with the Home and Colonial Government on account of the postal department, etc., not included in the "Home Charges." The shipment of stores in vessels chartered by Government do not figure in the statistics of Indian sea-borne trade as the vessels do not clear at the Customs. "In this way during the South African War and the China Expedition great quantities of material escaped record; much of this having been sold to the British Government represented a true commercial transaction affecting the balance of trade."[1] Credits to India on this account should have been properly included under commodity transactions. But in the absence of separate figures it could not be done. However, H. F. Howard has prepared an estimate of the value of such exports along with the credits and debits to India on account of the postal department, etc.—for money-order remittances sent to India from South Africa and elsewhere, which are honoured by the Indian Government in India, that Government being paid in London. As the credits and debits to India on account of the foreign money-order remittances have already been considered in the balance of non-commercial transactions, the adjustments with the Home Government on that account need not be considered again. Besides, the value of such adjustments is very small. Therefore, for the sake of this study, we accept H. F. Howard's estimate of the Miscellaneous Deposits and Remittances to be credited or debited to India without any allowance.

Table XVII represents the balance of India's credits and debits on account of railway annuities, India Bills, Movement of Securities, and the Miscellaneous Deposits and Remittances.

[1] *Report on the Operations of the Currency Department, 1913–14*, p. 48.

TABLE XVII*

BALANCE OF INDIA'S CREDITS AND DEBITS ON ACCOUNT OF RAILWAY ANNUITIES, INDIA BILLS, MOVEMENTS OF SECURITIES AND THE "MISCELLANEOUS DEPOSITS" AND REMITTANCES

(In lakhs of rupees)

	Credits				Debits					
Year	*India Bills*	*Securities Net*	*Miscellaneous Deposits and Remittances*†	*Total Credits*	*Railway Annuities and Sinking Fund*	*India Bills*	*Securities Net*	*Miscellaneous Deposits and Remittances*†	*Total Debits*	*Balance (Debits)*
1898–99	—	—	—	—	718	225	—	—	943	943
1899–00	—	—	157	157	739	—	65	—	804	647
1900–01	75	—	159	234	762	—	137	—	899	665
1901–02	—	—	264	264	780	150	181	—	1,111	847
1902–03	—	—	54	54	798	75	173	—	1,046	992
1903–04	—	—	319	319	799	225	149	—	1,173	854
1904–05	—	—	75	75	814	225	32	—	1,071	996
1905–06	—	—	29	29	756	75	38	—	870	841
1906–07	—	5	—	5	763	—	—	18	781	776
1907–08	150	—	94	244	738	—	126	—	864	620
1908–09	750	—	18	768	760	—	80	—	840	72
1909–10	—	78	—	78	789	—	—	52	841	763
1910–11	—	—	90	90	817	150	243	—	1,210	1,120
1911–12	—	—	73	73	823	75	106	—	1,004	931
1912–13	—	—	—	—	847	675	53	46	1,621	1,621
1913–14	—	112	168	280	826	—	—	—	826	546

* All the figures in this table, except those for "Miscellaneous Deposits and Remittances," are taken from *Statistical Abstracts for British India.*

† H. F. Howard, op. cit., pp. 66–67.

PRELIMINARY BALANCE OF INTERNATIONAL INDEBTEDNESS

We have now estimated the value of all classes of India's international transactions except interest payments on the amount of foreign capital invested in the country. The balance of India's international indebtedness in each year represents the net borrowing or lending of capital or the difference between its borrowings and loans. During the pre-war period the proverbially shy Indian capital is not known to have been seeking investment in foreign countries. Hence, if we tabulate all the items in our international transactions so far considered and strike balances between the credit and the debit items for each year during 1898–99 to 1913–14, the resulting figures would represent for each year the amount of foreign capital invested in India in that year minus the interest payments by India in that year on the total amount of foreign capital invested in India at the end of the preceding year. The results of this calculation are given in Table XVIII.

INTEREST PAYMENTS BY INDIA

The preliminary balance of indebtedness presented in Table XVIII represents the annual foreign borrowings of India minus the interest payments. If, therefore, we can reach an estimate of the interest charges payable by India every year during the period of our study it is quite possible to ascertain the actual amount of our foreign borrowings. To form an estimate of the interest charges payable by India, information on two points is necessary. Firstly, the total amount of foreign interest-bearing capital invested in India at the beginning of the period, i.e. at the beginning of the year 1898–99. Secondly, the rate of interest paid on the foreign capital invested in India before 1898–99 and the rates of interest paid for the subsequent years of our period. The sterling debt of India, which represents the foreign capital imported on Government account, stood at Rs. 18,490 lakhs in the beginning of the

TABLE XVIII

Preliminary Balance of International Indebtedness, 1898–1913

(In lakhs of rupees)

	Credits			Debits					
Year	Commodity Balance of Trade*	Credits on Account of Secretary of State's Balance†	Total Credits	Balance of Service Transactions‡	Balance of Non-Commercial Transactions§	Debits on Account of Secretary of State's Balance†	Railway Annuities, Etc.‖	Total Debits	Balance of Indebtedness (+ credit) (− debit)
1898–99	3,556	—	3,556	823	904	92	943	2,762	+ 794
1899–00	2,700	—	2,700	904	908	253	647	2,712	− 12
1900–01	2,291	111	2,402	933	861	—	665	2,459	− 57
1901–02	3,486	—	3,486	906	868	907	847	3,528	− 42
1902–03	3,575	85	3,660	1,050	875	—	992	2,917	+ 743
1903–04	4,534	—	4,534	1,034	871	613	854	3,372	+ 1,162
1904–05	3,854	—	3,854	1,059	871	746	996	3,672	+ 182
1905–06	3,283	—	3,283	1,137	862	1,534	841	4,374	− 1,091
1906–07	2,762	360	3,122	1,010	860	—	776	2,646	+ 476
1907–08	1,176	378	1,554	1,160	874	—	620	2,654	− 1,100
1908–09	1,732	789	2,521	1,270	912	—	72	2,254	+ 267
1909–10	4,220	—	4,220	1,162	907	2,124	763	4,956	− 736
1910–11	5,141	—	5,141	1,201	588	1,131	1,120	4,040	+ 1,101
1911–12	5,067	—	5,067	1,362	887	627	931	3,807	+ 1,260
1912–13	4,144	1,268	5,412	1,534	899	—	1,621	4,054	+ 1,358
1913–14	3,596	—	3,596	1,673	897	343	546	3,459	+ 137

* Supra, Table VI. † Supra, Table XVI. ‡ Supra, Table X. § Supra, Table XV. ‖ Supra, Table XVII.

year 1898–99, interest payments on which amounted to Rs. 582 lakhs annually. The total amount of non-Government borrowings at the beginning of the period was Rs. 20,863 lakhs, including private capital.[1]

About the rate of interest charged on the non-Government borrowings of India no reliable data are available. R. A. Lehfeldt,[2] from a careful study of the primary records, obtained the following average rates of interest at which "large"[3] colonial fixed income stocks were issued in Great Britain.

AVERAGE RATE OF RETURN ON LARGE COLONIAL INVESTMENTS ISSUED TO PAY A FIXED RATE OF INTEREST

Year	*Per cent*	*Year*	*Per cent*	*Year*	*Per cent*
1899	3·27	1904	3·78	1909	3·96
1900	3·20	1905	3·78	1910	4·19
1901	3·40	1906	3·85	1911	4·03
1902	3·21	1907	3·99	1912	4·30
1903	3·21	1908	4·04	1913	4·44

These averages relate to bond and preferred stock flotations, but do not include common stock issues. Lehfeldt,

[1] According to H. F. Howard's estimate the amount of British capital publicly invested in India on non-Government account was Rs. 21,150 lakhs at the end of 1910. Subtracting from this Rs. 8,653 lakhs, the amount of capital publicly invested in India from 1898 to 1910, we get Rs. 12,497 as the total amount of capital publicly invested in India at the end of 1897–98. According to Edgar Crammond the total British private investments abroad amounted to 27 per cent of its public investments in Government and non-Government securities. Taking this percentage to be true in the case of India we get Rs. 8,366 lakhs—27 per cent of Rs. 30,897 lakhs the total of British public investments in India at the end of 1897–98—as the total amount of foreign capital privately invested in India at the end of 1897–98. Hence the total of foreign non-Government public capital and private capital invested in India at the beginning of the period of our study is calculated to be Rs. 20,863 lakhs.

[2] R. A. Lehfeldt, "The Rate of Interest on British and Foreign Investments," 76. *Journal of the Royal Statistical Society, 1912–13.*

[3] Issues of cash value exceeding £900,000.

however, discovered in the course of his study that common stock issues were only 10 per cent of the total British investments in large issues and that the percentage was lower still if only the investments outside Great Britain were taken into account. Hence the accuracy of these averages as far as they go suffers only slightly by the exclusion of common stock issues. In the year 1902 the average rate of return on large fixed-income Indian Stock was 2·95 per cent, lower than the average of all colonial fixed-income issues by 0·26 per cent. This suggests that the average rates of interest on colonial fixed-income issues obtained by Lehfeldt are a little higher than what they might have been for India alone. But as against this, there is the consideration that the average rate of interest on India Stock represents an average of the rates of interest on Government and non-Government borrowings. Government loans, however, are floated at lower rates of interest than the non-Government loans and, as such, the average rates on colonial fixed-income issues may approximately represent the rates charged on Indian non-Government issues. In the absence of better information, we ignore the fact that according to Lehfeldt the Indian non-Government issues were for the most part of the "medium"[1] category, while the averages of rates of interest quoted above refer to "large" issues and make use of them to estimate the interest charges payable on the foreign non-Government borrowings of India after 1898–99. Similarly, though Lehfeldt's average rates of interest are higher than the rates at which Government loans were raised in London, to facilitate the use of the method described in the following paragraph for ascertaining India's balance of indebtedness, we apply them also to the Government borrowings after 1898–99. Allowance for the error resulting from the application of higher rates of interest will be made in the next chapter. Taking into consideration that the interest rates were at an unusually low level in the last decade of the nine-

[1] Issues whose cash value was between £100,000 and £900,000.

teenth century, we take 3 per cent to be the approximate rate of interest paid by India on the total amount of her non-Government borrowings effected prior to 1898–99.[1]

At 3 per cent the interest paid by India on Rs. 20,863 lakhs, the total of her non-Government borrowings in the beginning of 1898–99, amounted to Rs. 625 lakhs. In the same year the amount of interest charges paid on Government account was Rs. 582 lakhs. As against this, India received a small sum of Rs. 4 lakhs on the investments of the Secretary of State's reserves and cash balances in London. Therefore the total of net interest charges paid by India in 1898–99 works out at Rs. 1,207 lakhs. Table XVIII represents India's balance of indebtedness for each year, but with interest payments unaccounted for. Subtraction of the preliminary credit balance of India in 1898–99 from the interest payments by India for that year will as a result give us the amount of foreign capital invested in India in that year. In the calculation of interest payments for each subsequent year there must be included the interest on foreign capital invested in India from the beginning of 1898–99 to the end of the year preceding. The "net"[2] investment of foreign capital in India in each year during the period of our study can then be ascertained by adding as debits the net interest payments by India during the corresponding year to the preliminary balances of indebtedness worked out in Table XVIII.

The annual net interest payments by India and the annual

[1] In the year 1898 the average rate of interest earned by large Colonial fixed-income issues was 3·07 per cent. However, the course of interest was declining until the middle of the last decade of the nineteenth century. Therefore the interest earned by the investments made prior to 1898 can be reasonably expected to be lower than 3·07 per cent. We have taken it exactly at three for the sake of convenience.

Cf. Viner's *Canada's Balance of International Indebtedness, 1900–13*, p. 99.

[2] I.e. the excess of new investments over liquidation of old investments.

TABLE XIX

Foreign Capital Investments in India and Interest Payments

(In lakhs of rupees)

Year	Balance of Indebtedness from Table XVIII (+ credit) (− debit) I	Interest Payments on Capital Invested in India: Before 1898* II	From 1898 to Year Previous to Given Year† III	Credits to India on Account of the Money Deposited in Short-Term Securities in London‡ IV	Net Total Payments by India (II + III + IV) V	Capital Investments in India in each Year (I + V) VI	Total Capital Invested in India from 1898 to Year Previous to Given Year VII
1898–99	+ 794	1,207	—	4	1,203	409	—
1899–00	− 12	1,207	13	7	1,213	1,225	409
1900–01	− 57	1,207	52	8	1,251	1,308	1,634
1901–02	− 42	1,207	99	11	1,295	1,337	2,922
1902–03	+ 743	1,207	136	23	1,320	577	4,259
1903–04	+ 1,162	1,207	155	21	1,341	179	4,826
1904–05	+ 182	1,207	189	24	1,372	1,190	5,005
1905–06	− 1,091	1,207	234	35	1,406	2,497	6,195
1906–07	+ 476	1,207	335	37	1,505	1,029	8,692
1907–08	− 1,100	1,207	388	27	1,568	2,668	9,721
1908–09	+ 267	1,207	501	13	1,695	1,428	12,389
1909–10	− 736	1,207	547	25	1,729	2,465	13,827
1910–11	+ 1,101	1,207	683	61	1,829	728	16,292
1911–12	+ 1,260	1,207	686	68	1,825	565	17,019
1912–13	+ 1,358	1,207	756	70	1,893	535	17,584
1913–14	+ 137	1,207	804	47	1,964	1,827	18,119

* At the rate of 3 per cent per annum.

† At the rates of interest calculated by Lehfeldt.

‡ Figures taken from the *Statistical Abstracts for British India.*

net investments of foreign capital in India as calculated by the method explained in the preceding paragraph are summarized in Table XIX.

In calculating the interest payments we have used the figures

TABLE XX

BALANCE OF SERVICE TRANSACTIONS

(In lakhs of rupees)

Year	*Freight Payment by India** I	*Insurance, Banking, and Other Minor Charges†* II	*Home Charges‡* III	*Net Interest Payments§* IV	*Balance of Service Transactions* (I+II+III+IV) *(Debit)* V
1898–99	392	198	233	1,203	2,026
1899–00	457	230	217	1,213	2,117
1900–01	479	248	206	1,251	2,184
1901–02	570	249	87	1,295	2,201
1902–03	572	247	231	1,320	2,370
1903–04	559	291	184	1,341	2,375
1904–05	572	316	171	1,372	2,431
1905–06	659	334	144	1,406	2,543
906–07	476	362	172	1,505	2,515
1907–08	582	395	183	1,568	2,728
1908–09	687	357	226	1,695	2,965
1909–10	572	386	204	1,729	2,891
1910–11	554	425	222	1,829	3,030
1911–12	683	461	218	1,825	3,187
1912–13	903	414	217	1,893	3,427
1913–14	1,030	423	220	1,964	3,637

* Supra, Table VII. † Supra, Table VIII.
‡ Supra, Table IX. § Supra, Table XIX.

published in the *Financial Statistics of British India* for interest charges on the total amount of Government borrowing prior to 1898. For the Government and non-Government borrowings after 1898 we have made use of Lehfeldt's average rates of interest on colonial fixed-income issues, and the estimate of 3 per cent is used for the non-Government borrowings effected before 1898–99.

CHAPTER V

CAPITAL INVESTMENTS IN INDIA—A VERIFICATION

By a roundabout process we have arrived at the probable amount of capital invested in India during the period 1898–99 to 1913–14. The calculation is based on the assumption that the immediate debit and credit obligations of a country balance one another during a year. No abstruse argument is needed to justify this assumption. When, therefore, all the items except foreign investments[1] entering into the balance sheet of India have been evaluated, the excess of debits or credits revealed must naturally be due to net foreign borrowing or lending. If we can now secure a direct verification of this indirect estimate of foreign capital investments in India during the period of our study, we shall incidentally construct an effective test of the accuracy or otherwise of the values assigned to the invisible items. In the following pages we make such an attempt.

STATISTICS OF INTERNATIONAL INVESTMENTS

During the pre-war period almost all the capital imported for the development of this country was received from Great Britain. There is a considerable amount of statistical data relating to the investment of such capital in India. But while handling the statistical information one has to be cautious. In the first place much of the available information is of questionable accuracy, and that which can be considered as accurate fails to cover the entire period of our study. Besides, statistics of foreign investments display certain characteristic features

[1] C. K. Hobson defines foreign investments as that part of the property of a country and its inhabitants which is situated abroad and from which its owners expect to derive an income. *Export of Capital*, p. 1.

which make it difficult, if not impossible, to arrive at an accurate and complete estimate of such investments in India. For certain classes of investments statistical information cannot be secured at all.

So far as Great Britain's public investments in India are concerned, there are some reliable compilations, but they relate only to a few stray years. There is scattered information on this point available in the issues of the *Economist* for the whole period of our study. However, in using the compilations made even by reliable and competent authorities and in preparing new ones a certain amount of caution is necessary. First, the term "public investments" is applied to all the capital investments made through the issue of securities for public sale after advertisement in financial journals. These securities are almost invariably issued through brokers and agents in the capital market. It is, therefore, essential to know whether the compilations of such issues refer to nominal or par values or are based on the actual issue prices of the securities, as the results obtained for common shares will differ appreciably according to the method used. For fixed-income securities and common stock, compilations based on issue price are preferable for our present purpose, which is to ascertain India's balance of indebtedness during the pre-war period of the gold-exchange standard. On the other hand, in the case of bonds and debenture stocks, par values can be used in preference. For share securities, which do not involve any contractual obligation about the repayment of the principal at some definite future date, it is debatable which method of compilation will yield reliable and satisfactory results. Nevertheless, in order to ascertain the actual flow of capital into India we have followed Viner,[1] and used issue price for all classes of securities except the Government and Railway securities whose nominal value alone is recorded in the *Financial Statistics* of the Government, which form an im-

[1] J. Viner, op. cit., p. 109.

portant source of our information. From the issue price we have also deducted the shares of the vendor and the promoter.

Secondly, when a loan is simultaneously floated in different countries the total issue may be recorded in the compilations of all the markets. So also, when a loan is raised in one country a part of the securities might subsequently travel to another country through private dealings on the Stock Exchange and may figure in the estimates of one country as public investments and of another as private investments. In both these cases the amount of a country's borrowings is likely to be greatly exaggerated. However, the magnitude of Indian indebtedness in particular will not be seriously affected by these duplications in the statistics of international investments. First, because we know that almost all of our foreign obligations are held by Britishers. Our loans in the pre-war period were opened for subscription only in the London Money Market. Secondly, the published statistics of foreign investments in India relate only to public investments, so that even if a portion of one country's public investments in India reappeared as the private investments of another, the fact would not affect the true estimate of India's foreign borrowings.

Thirdly, a confusion between the amount of loans authorized and the amount actually issued provides a further source of error. At times, if an issue is under-subscribed, the unsubscribed part is withdrawn and reissued on better terms for the investor. The double inclusion of the reissued part in such a case must be avoided. Similarly, care must be taken to see that conversion loans and new issues made to liquidate maturing obligations are not included in any compilation of foreign investments. During the period of our study, however, not a single conversion loan was floated on behalf of India.

GREAT BRITAIN'S PUBLIC INVESTMENTS IN INDIA

For the Sterling Loans of the Government we have used the figures compiled by the Department of Statistics in

India.[1] These represent the net amount of capital floated every year in the London Money Market on Government account. Besides these loans, which constitute the Public Debt of India,

TABLE XXII

PUBLIC INVESTMENTS OF BRITISH CAPITAL IN INDIA EVERY YEAR DURING THE PERIOD 1898–99 TO 1913–14

(In lakhs of rupees)

Year	*Net Amount of Sterling Loans Raised by the Government**	*Other Loans Publicly Raised in London†*	*Total Amount of Loans Publicly Raised in London*
1898–99	149	375	524
1899–00	– 18	405	387
1900–01	1,393	855	2,248
1901–02	131	240	371
1902–03	423	360	783
1903–04	– 612	315	– 297
1904–05	– 23	570	547
1905–06	2,035	525	2,560
1906–07	160	75	235
1907–08	1,344	300‡	1,644
1908–09	673	1,374	2,047
1909–10	1,370	1,027	2,397
1910–11	1,184	1,032	2,216
1911–12	73	529	602
1912–13	105	455	560
1913–14	– 317	785	468

* Sterling figures converted at 1s. 4d. per rupee. *Statistics of British India*, vol. iii, Financial Statistics, Nominal Value.

† Figures collected from the volumes of the *Economist* represent issue price.

‡ Taken from the Report of the Controller of Currency, 1913–14, p. 53.

there are others raised by the big industrial concerns and commercial enterprises carrying on their business in India. We have collected information about the capital raised abroad by such concerns from the issues of the *Economist*. For the

[1] These figures are published in the *Statistics of British India*, vol. iii, Financial Statistics.

year 1907–8 figures of the *Economist* could not be obtained, and hence we have used the estimate of the annual flow of such loans prepared by H. F. Howard. This estimate has been more fully dealt with elsewhere. While collecting the data from the volumes of the *Economist* we have taken account of the amount of loans actually issued at their issue price and not of the nominal value of the loans authorized. By adding up the two sets of figures for Government and private borrowings thus collected, we have arrived at the net amount of capital publicly floated in London, every year, on behalf of India. The results are presented in Table XXII.

We see from the table that the Indian borrowings in London amounted to Rs. 17,292 lakhs during the period 1898–99 to 1913–14. The years 1900–1, 1905–6, and 1907–8 to 1910–11 were years of particularly heavy borrowings, and except in the year 1903–4 we had a credit balance of payment on capital account in all years. We shall now examine how far these figures are correct in the light of investigations made by some eminent statisticians to arrive at the magnitude of British investments in India.

I. EDGAR CRAMMOND'S ESTIMATE[1]

In 1907 Edgar Crammond made an estimate of the total amount of British capital invested in foreign countries and colonies till the end of 1906. Some years afterwards the estimate was brought up to the end of 1910. In his estimate Crammond has given the amount of British capital absorbed by every individual country and colony. Besides the main purpose of Crammond's investigation being to prove the prosperity of British investments abroad, he has also given similar figures for the years 1896 and 1897. From this estimate we get the total amounts of British capital invested in India at the end of 1896, 1897, 1906, and 1910.

[1] Edgar Crammond, "British Investments Abroad," *Quarterly Review*, July 1907 and July 1911.

The sources on which Crammond relies for his information are: The Official List of the London Stock Exchange, the Official Lists issued by Provincial Stock Exchanges, and the Stock Exchange Official Intelligence.[1] For calculating the amount of British capital invested in India he takes into consideration the value of Indian securities quoted in the

TABLE XXIII

E. CRAMMOND'S ESTIMATE OF BRITISH CAPITAL INVESTED IN INDIA AND CEYLON

*(In lakhs of rupees)**

Year†	1896	1897	1906	1910
Government Stock	—	15,900	19,140	—
Railways	—	14,010	19,440	—
Corporation Stock, Banking, Financial, Land, etc.	—	750	1,200	—
Mines	—	210	345	—
Miscellaneous	—	3,900	6,000	—
Total	44,100	34,770‡	46,125	64,500

* Original figures are in millions of £s. We have converted them at 1s. 4d. per rupee.

† Calendar Year.

‡ The figure appears to be incorrect inasmuch as it suggests that British capital worth Rs. 9,330 lakhs was withdrawn from India during the year 1897–98. Never in the history of British capital investments in India has such a large amount of capital been withdrawn from India during a single year.

Stock Exchange Official Intelligence, which includes the securities quoted in the other two lists. This method cannot be applied to estimate the amount of capital employed by British companies in carrying on their business in India. The capital of such concerns is therefore completely excluded by Crammond from his estimate. The figures of British capital investments in India and Ceylon according to Crammond are given in Table XXIII.

[1] This valuable document contains particulars of all the companies, home and foreign, whose securities are dealt in or known on any of the Stock Exchanges of the United Kingdom.

II. SIR GEORGE PAISH'S ESTIMATE OF BRITISH INVESTMENTS IN INDIA

In the same way as Crammond, Sir George Paish, while calculating the total amount of British capital exported, incidentally gives figures for India's indebtedness to Great Britain on capital account. He supplies two sets of data. From his first estimate which was embodied in the papers he read before the Royal Statistical Society we get the total amount of capital imported from Great Britain into this country till the year 1910.[1] In addition, we also find figures of loans raised for individual years during the period 1906 to 1910, but they relate only to loans floated on behalf of the Government, the Municipalities, and the Railways. His second compilation, which covers the period 1908 to 1913, is more comprehensive.[2] It gives the total amount of loans incurred on behalf of India in Great Britain for every year during the period.

For the major part of his information he relies on the Reports of the Inland Revenue Commissioners. These reports contain particulars of the income derived by British investors from abroad which is disclosed for the purpose of taxation. The income so earmarked comprises the following heads:[3]

Income disclosed by agents for payment of interest on foreign and colonial Government securities.

Income disclosed by agents for payment of dividends and interest of foreign and colonial companies and corporations.

Income disclosed by bankers and coupon-dealers in connection with the realization of foreign and colonial coupons.

Income declared by persons, firms, or public companies as received

[1] Sir G. Paish, "Great Britain's Investments in Other Lands," *Journal of the Royal Statistical Society*, September 1909; "Great Britain's Investments in Individual Colonies and Foreign Countries,' ibid., January 1911.

[2] The *Statist*, February 14, 1914.

[3] 53. Inland Revenue Report, p. 128. Quoted by Crammond, *Quarterly Review*, July 1911, p. 44.

in respect of investments abroad without taxation at the hands of agents, bankers, or coupon-dealers.

Profits of those railways abroad which are owned and worked by British companies with the seat of management in the United Kingdom.

The commissioners, however, point out that besides the earnings coming under these earmarked heads there exists a large amount of income which cannot be assigned to any particular head in the absence of information which the tax-payer alone can submit. Such unidentified income they include under the general category of "business, professions, etc., not otherwise detailed." It includes the profits derived from the following sources:[1]

Concerns—other than railways—situated abroad but having their seat of direction and management in the United Kingdom, e.g. mines, gasworks, waterworks, tramways, breweries, tea, coffee, and rubber plantations, nitrate grounds, oil fields, land and financial companies, etc.

Concerns jointly worked abroad and in the United Kingdom, such as electric telegraph cables and shipping.

Foreign and colonial branches of banks, insurance companies, and mercantile houses in the United Kingdom.

Mortgages of property and other loans and deposits abroad belonging to banks, insurance companies, land mortgage and financial companies, etc., in this country.

Profits of all kinds arising from business done abroad by manufacturers, merchants, and commission agents resident in the United Kingdom.

Sir G. Paish does not take account of the income from the last four sources but amplifies the information on the first source of income contained in the commissioners' reports by examining the reports, balance-sheets, and income statements of several thousand companies.[2] The profits earned by the

[1] C. K. Hobson, *The Export of Capital*, p. 200.

[2] "In fact, I have examined the reports of all British companies working abroad about which official information could be obtained." Sir G. Paish, *Journal of the Royal Statistical Society*, vol. 74, part ii, p. 167.

latter are added to the amount of income from foreign investments assessed to income-tax in the reports of the Revenue Commissioners. The total income is then capitalized on a yield basis of 5·2 per cent. To arrive at the amount of capital investments in individual countries and colonies different rates of capitalization are used. According to this estimate the total amount of British capital publicly invested in India and Ceylon at the end of 1910 was as follows:

TABLE XXIV*

BRITISH INVESTMENTS IN INDIA AND CEYLON AT THE END OF 1910†

	(*Rs.* 100,000)‡
Government	26,850
Railways	20,475
Corporation Stocks, Banking, Financial, Land, etc.	1,320
Mines	525
Miscellaneous	5,610
Total	54,780

* Compiled from the figures published in the *Royal Statistical Society's Journal*, vol. 74, p. 180.

† Nominal value.

‡ The original figures in £s are converted at 1s. 4d. for a rupee.

Sir George Paish, however, confesses that the figures calculated by him are an under-statement. Mr. Henry Beaumont emphasized the same point in the course of the discussion on Sir G. Paish's papers[1] at the Statistical Society. Paish's compilation of British capital invested in India and Ceylon for every year during the period 1908 to 1913 is presented in Table XXV.

The figures in Columns II and III for the years 1908, 1909, and 1910 do not agree though compiled by the same authority.

[1] *Journal of the Royal Statistical Society*, vol. 72, Discussion, p. 483.

For this no other reason can be assigned but some omission in the first set of figures compiled in 1910. The difference appears to be rather serious for the year 1910. We shall, however, accept the figures in Column III as more accurate, being the later.

TABLE XV*

ESTIMATE OF BRITISH CAPITAL INVESTED IN INDIA AND CEYLON EVERY YEAR DURING THE PERIOD 1908 to 1913 ACCORDING TO SIR G. PAISH

(In lakhs of rupees)†

Year	*The Amount of British Capital Invested in India and Ceylon*‡	
I	II	III
1908	2,020§	1,965
1909	2,383	2,295
1910	2,208	2,700
1911	—	765
1912	—	555
1913	—	570

* Compiled from the information supplied by the London *Statist* dated February 14, 1914, and the *Journal of the Royal Statistical Society*, vol. 74.

† The original figures in £s converted at 1s. 4d. per rupee.

‡ The figures exclude conversion loans and vendors' shares and represent issue price.

§ *Journal of the Royal Statistical Society*, vol. 74, p. 172.

III. THE EXTENT OF BRITISH CAPITAL IN INDIA:[1] H. F. HOWARD

Unlike the last two estimates H. F. Howard's estimate relates exclusively to India and supplies information both for the total amount of British investments in India at the end of 1910 and for individual years during the period 1899 to 1913. However, Howard does not give any information about the sources of his data bearing on the probable amount of capital imported by India. He starts with the Government of India loans, which

[1] H. F. Howard, *India and the Gold Exchange Standard*, p. 92.

cover by far the largest portion of capital imported into the country and which largely represent productive expenditure on railways and irrigation works. These loans, which amounted to Rs. 31,500 lakhs at the end of 1910, he assigns entirely to British investors. The outstanding railway annuities, which amounted approximately to Rs. 10,950 lakhs, are also taken into account. Next to Government of India loans are the loans floated in the open market in London by local bodies in India. The total amount of these loans on March 31, 1910, was about Rs. 3,600 lakhs.[1] Allowing for the fact that a large portion of these loans is held by the natives of India, the Controller of Currency estimates Rs. 1,500 lakhs as the share of English investors. He does not give any reasons for the assignment of this share only. The stock of public companies is the third important item. At the end of 1908–9 the paid-up capital of the companies registered in India was Rs. 6,550 lakhs. Much of this was invested in mills or presses mainly for pressing cotton, jute, wool, and silk.[2] Allowing for the share of Indian investors, which was not small, Howard puts Rs. 3,000 lakhs as the amount of British capital under this head. Here, again, the division of shares between Indian and British capital seems to be wholly arbitrary. In the case of companies with a sterling capital doing their business more or less exclusively in India, almost the whole of it is taken to be of British origin. By the close of the year referred to above the capital of these companies amounted to Rs. 10,350 lakhs and the debentures to Rs. 6,300 lakhs, making Rs. 16,650 lakhs in all. To these figures Howard adds Rs. 3,900 lakhs on account of the "English Banking, Loan, and Insurance Capital employed in India." This takes into account the class of public companies registered outside India and doing only a small part of their business in this country. Bringing together all these items we get the total

[1] H. F. Howard, *India and the Gold Exchange Standard*, p. 93.

[2] The figures exclude the capital of the Presidency Banks, which amounted to Rs. 360 lakhs.

amount of British capital invested in India at the end of 1910, as follows:

	*In Lakhs of Rs.**
Government loans	31,500
Railway annuities	10,950
Loans of local bodies	1,500
Companies registered in India	3,000
Companies with a sterling capital	16,650
Banking, Insurance, etc.	3,900
Total Rs.	67,500

* Sterling figures converted at 1s. 4d. per rupee and represent nominal value.

Mr. Howard's estimate of British capital imported into India every year from 1899–1900 to 1913–14 is based on more reliable data. He collects the relevant figures under four heads: net debt incurred at London on behalf of the India Government, net capital deposited by railway companies with the Secretary of State, capital borrowed by Port Trusts and other capital loaned to India. Net capital deposited by railway companies excludes the capital raised by the Bengal and North-Western Railway "in which Government have no direct financial concern." The last heading, "other capital loaned to India," requires some explanation. Besides the Government of India, Railways, and Port Trusts, there were private firms who raised loans in the London Money Market by issuing public securities. Every year there was some import of capital into India on this account and this is put under the category "other capital, etc." Howard arrives at an approximate figure of these loans on the basis of information published by the Indian Commercial Intelligence Department to show the capital of sterling companies working exclusively in India. The tables relate to the period 1905–6 to 1909–10. He concludes: "Excluding the railway figures the capital loaned to British India increased during the period from £26 to over

£40 millions, of which about £5¾ millions were invested in tea, £4 millions in navigation, and £3 millions in jute. This increase is at the rate of £3 millions a year.[1] He assumes the figure of the new loans made to India by the London Money

TABLE XXVI*

THE ANNUAL NON-GOVERNMENT EXTERNAL BORROWING BY INDIA ACCORDING TO H. F. HOWARD, 1899–1900 TO 1913–14

(*In lakhs of rupees*)†

Year‡	*Port Trust Borrowings*	*Other Capital Raised by non-Government Concerns in India*
1899–00	—	300
1900–01	—	300
1901–02	—	300
1902–03	—	300
1903–04	—	300
1904–05	—	300
1905–06	—	300
1906–07	—	300
1907–08	—	300
1908–09	—	300
1909–10	150	285§
1910–11	315	585§
1911–12	120	165§
1912–13	—	165§
1913–14	—	105§

* Compiled from the figures given in Appendix I, *Report of the Controller of Currency*, 1913–14.

† Sterling figures converted at 1s. 4d. per rupee.

‡ Indian fiscal year—from the 1st of April to 31st of March.

§ Figures compiled from the issues of the *Economist* refer to calendar years.

Market to be £2 millions for every year during the period prior to 1909–10. For the rest of the period he has corrected this average in the light of the information supplied by the *Economist*. As we have already collected from an authoritative

[1] *Report on the Operations of the Currency Department, 1913–14*, p. 52.

Government publication the information about Government and Railway loans, Table XXVI represents an estimate of India's non-Government borrowings according to Howard.

LIMITATIONS OF THE PRECEDING ESTIMATES

The estimates of the total amount of British capital investments made by Edgar Crammond and Sir George Paish do not refer to India alone but to India and Ceylon together. Naturally this exaggerates the amount of British capital invested in India by the amount of British capital invested in Ceylon.

As a partial off-set against this over-estimate we may take into account the fact that Crammond and Paish do not take into account the capital employed in India by the British shipping companies, telegraph, insurance, and other companies whose head offices are situated in Great Britain.[1] This omission is likely to introduce a large margin of error in an estimate of the total amount of British capital invested in India, because the Exchange Banks and the Shipping companies engaged in the coastal trade of India with their head offices in London are supposed to employ a large amount of their capital in this country.

In addition to this omission, which is common to both these estimates, there are some other points which tend to undermine the accuracy of Paish's estimate in particular. Sir George Paish has formed his estimate of Government loans by

[1] "It is necessary to obtain a comprehensive idea as to the amount of British capital employed or invested abroad to make a further addition in respect of the capital engaged by British shipping employed in the colonial and foreign carrying trades and also of the capital represented by the telegraph, insurance, and other companies carrying on business partly in the United Kingdom and partly in the colonies and foreign countries, which cannot, of course, be geographically apportioned."—E. Crammond, *Quarterly Review*, July 1907, p. 253.

Vide Sir G. Paish, *Journal of the Royal Statistical Society*, vol. 74, p. 187.

capitalizing the income received by British holders of Indian Government securities as reported to the British Income Tax authorities, and of the loans taken by Indian Corporations by an examination of individual company reports. But the income actually received by British investors in a particular year may not represent all the income to which they may be entitled.[1] In fact, a portion of that income is never brought to the Home Country, but is reinvested in India. This portion, therefore, escapes capitalization in the year the computation is made. Secondly, there is a small amount of British capital invested in India which does not bring any income to the investor.[2] The method of capitalization adopted by Paish cannot take any cognizance of this amount also. True, our balance of payments is not affected by such investments so far as the payment of interest is concerned, because either they do not bear any interest or the interest is not transmitted abroad. But the balance of payments must have been affected by the import of this capital, in the year in which such imports took place.

H. F. Howard's estimate, on the other hand, is free from all the criticism directed against the other two estimates. It refers to British capital investment in India alone and includes in its purview even the class of capital which does not yield any interest. Moreover, Howard also makes some allowance for the capital of the Exchange Banks, Shipping Companies, etc., which were registered in London and which carried on a good deal of business in India. But the greatest defect of his estimate is that it is largely a guesswork. A large amount of capital employed in India is assigned to Great Britain without any statistical evidence. Besides, the estimate is also theoreti-

[1] "As a matter of fact a large part of the income earned by British capital invested abroad was never brought home but was reinvested in the country from which it was derived." *Journal of the Royal Statistical Society*, vol. 72, p. 482.

[2] Ibid., vol. 74, p. 192.

cally defective on one point; it includes the share of India's internal debt held by Europeans in India. As a matter of fact, the capital invested by Europeans in rupee securities is not imported from Great Britain and, as such, should be omitted from an estimate of the total amount of British capital invested in this country. By the term "British Investments" we mean capital flowing to India from Great Britain and not the amount of capital invested in India by Europeans staying in India. For the sake of comparison we give below all the three estimates of the total amount of British capital invested in India at the end of 1910–11:[1]

(*In lakhs of Rs.*)

E. Crammond	64,500	India and Ceylon
Sir G. Paish	54,780	India and Ceylon
H. F. Howard	63,000[2]	India

We think that Crammond's estimate is more correct than the other two inasmuch as it is based on actual data and takes account of all the classes of British investments in India except Banking, Insurance, and Shipping capital. To make the actual results more comparable, we omit from Howard's estimate Rs. 3,900 lakhs, the capital of the Exchange Banks and the Shipping companies which is not included in the other two estimates. Howard's figure for British investments in India, then, stands at Rs. 59,100 lakhs. This is certainly higher than the estimate of Sir George Paish, which is admittedly an under-estimate. On the other hand, it is lower than Crammond's estimate by Rs. 5,400 lakhs. This difference, however, may be due to the inclusion of British investments in Ceylon by Crammond. We may, therefore, say that the

[1] Calendar Year.

[2] After making allowance for the inclusion in his original estimate of Rs. 4,500 lakhs on account of the internal rupee debt held by Europeans in India.

estimates of British investments in India prepared by Crammond and Howard are approximately correct as far as they go.

VERIFICATION OF TABLE XXII

At the end of the year 1896 the amount of British investments in India according to Crammond was Rs. 44,100 lakhs. It went up to Rs. 64,500 lakhs by the end of the year 1910. This means that British capital worth about Rs. 20,400 lakhs was invested in India during the period 1896 to 1910. According to our estimate, which is presented in Table XXII, the amount of British capital invested in India during the period 1898–99 to 1913–14 was Rs. 17,292 lakhs. During the common period 1898–99 to 1910–11, the total amount of British capital invested in India, according to Crammond, was Rs. 18,570 lakhs, while according to our calculation the figure works out at Rs. 15,662 lakhs.[1] The excess of Rs. 2,908 lakhs which is shown by Crammond's estimate is most probably due to his inclusion of British capital invested in Ceylon. Therefore, so far as the total amount of British capital imported into India during the period of our study is concerned, our estimate is approximately correct. To ascertain the accuracy of our figures representing the annual flow of this capital we bring together the relevant data in Table XXVII.

The figures of loans raised on behalf of the Government, which are taken from the *Financial Statistics of India*, itself a Government publication, need no verification. In the case of non-Government loans we find that Howard's figures, which

[1] To arrive at these figures we have deducted from E. Crammond's figure for the total amount of British capital invested in India during 1896–97 to 1910–11 the amount of British capital invested in India during the years 1896–97 and 1897–98, which comes to about Rs. 1,830 lakhs, and from our estimate, which covers the period 1898–99 to 1913–14, a similar allowance has been made for the amount of British capital invested in India during the years 1911–12, 1912–13, and 1913–14, which works out at Rs. 1,630 lakhs.

TABLE XXVII

THE INFLOW OF BRITISH CAPITAL TO INDIA EVERY YEAR DURING 1898–99 TO 1913–14

(*In lakhs of rupees*)

	The Present Estimate*			Howard's Estimate†	Sir G. Paish's Estimate‡
Year	*Net Amount of Sterling Loans Raised by the Government*	*Other Loans Publicly Raised in London*	*Total*	*Loans other than those on Government Account Publicly Raised in London*	*Net Amount of British Capital Invested in India*
1898–99	149	375	524	—	—
1899–00	— 18	405	387	—	—
1900–01	1,393	855	2,248	300	—
1901–02	131	240	371	300	—
1902–03	423	360	783	300	—
1903–04	— 612	315	— 297	300	—
1904–05	— 23	570	547	300	—
1905–06	2,035	525	2,560	300	—
1906–07	160	75	235	300	—
1907–08	1,344	300	1,644	300	—
1908–09	673	1,374	2,047	300	2,047
1909–10	1,370	1,027	2,397	435	2,397
1910–11	1,184	1,032	2,216	900	2,216
1911–12	73	529	602	285	712
1912–13	105	455	560	165	559
1913–14	— 317	785	468	105	468

* Table XXII. † Table XXVI. ‡ Calendar year figures in Table XXV adjusted to the Indian Fiscal Year basis.

are the only figures available for comparison, are throughout lower than the figures compiled by us except for the years 1901–2 and 1906–7. We, however, know that Howard calculated the average amount of sterling capital raised by non-Government concerns at Rs. 450 lakhs every year, during the period 1905–6 to 1909–10 and brought it down to Rs. 300 lakhs so as to make it applicable to the period 1899–1900 to 1913–14 as a whole. He has not assigned any reason whatsoever for lowering the average to Rs. 300 lakhs for the earlier years. Later on he made some corrections in this general average for the period 1908–9 to 1913–14, but on the whole his figures appear to be somewhat arbitrary and unreliable. On the other hand, our figures for the total amount of British capital imported into India are largely in agreement with the figures of Sir George Paish which are compiled from the information provided by the *Economist*. The close approximation between these two sets of figures bears out their correctness. Therefore, according to all the available evidence, our estimate of the amount of British capital publicly invested both for individual years as well as for the period as a whole is approximately correct.

BRITISH PRIVATE INVESTMENTS IN INDIA

Besides public investments in India, made through the issue of securities for public sale, there are other investments on private account. They take a great number of forms and receive very little publicity. If such investments are made by the private sale of securities they may be divided into two classes: first, sales by issuing Governments or Corporations, of entire issues or large blocks of new issues at the time of issue, direct to investment companies or to syndicates of private investors; and second, the transfer of small lots of Indian securities from Indian to British ownership in the ordinary course of stock-exchange transactions. But the private purchase of Indian securities is only one of the methods by which private capital is invested in India, and as we have said before, private investments in India assume many other forms. These include: the investments of British insurance companies in India; British purchases of Indian mining, agricultural, and urban interests; the investments of British shipping companies in Indian coastwise shipping; direct investments in Indian industrial plants and mercantile establishments, and British capital used in financing Indian import and export trade.

It is impossible, however, to get any information bearing directly on the volume of such investments in India. Hence resort must necessarily be taken to indirect methods which might yield some rough estimate. Edgar Crammond has estimated the total amount of British investments abroad, both public and private separately, at the end of the years 1897, 1906, and 1910. The percentages of the total amount of private investments to the total of public investments at the end of these years were 27, 20, and 14 respectively.[1] According to Sir George Paish this percentage relation between the totals of British public and private investments was reduced by 1·5 during 1910 to 1913,[2] and though his absolute figures are an under-estimate they may be taken as a fairly accurate index of a trend. So it means that at the end of 1913 the percentage was 12·5. The decrease of private investments relatively to public investments is due not only to the increase

[1] *(In lakhs of rupees)*

Year	*Total Amount of Great Britain's Public Investments* I	*Total Amount of Great Britain's Private Investments* II	*Percentage of* II *to* I
1897	2,82,900	77,100	27
1906	3,93,000	79,500	20
1910	4,90,800	67,500	14

[2] The figures of Sir G. Paish show that the percentage relation between Public and Private Investments was 9 at the end of 1910 and 7·5 at the end of 1913.

of Great Britain's public investments abroad during the period, but also to the absolute decrease in the total amount of private investments themselves. "The tendency lately with regard to enterprises abroad had been to turn them into companies."[1] New investments of private capital directly by the investor or through mercantile and banking houses were diminishing year by year, while the old investments were being gradually transformed into public investments by the conversion of private securities into public securities and private enterprises into companies. The net result of this process of transformation can be discerned in the very slight increase of Rs. 2,400 lakhs, i.e. 3 per cent in the total amount of British private investments during the period 1897 to 1906 and in the decrease of Rs. 12,000 lakhs, i.e. 15 per cent during 1906 to 1910. The figures of Sir G. Paish show that this tendency of private investments to decrease continued till the end of 1913. The slight increase in the total amount of British private investments abroad during 1897 to 1906 may very likely be due to the impetus they received from the heavy outburst of public investments since 1904. But the impetus seems to have lasted only for a short time.

On the supposition that the percentage relation between the total amount of Great Britain's public and private investments abroad is true also in the case of India taken separately, we have calculated the total amount of British private investments in India at the end of 1897, 1906, 1910, and 1913. For the remaining years covered by the period of our study our calculations are based on the assumption of equal annual distribution of the difference in these percentages. The results are represented in Table XXVIII.

According to this estimate, during the period 1898–99 to 1913–14, private capital worth Rs. 2,293 lakhs was withdrawn from India or converted into public securities. The

[1] Sir R. B. Martin, "Discussion on Sir G. Paish's paper, *Journal of the Royal Statistical Society*, vol. 72, p. 486.

TABLE XXVIII

GREAT BRITAIN'S PRIVATE INVESTMENTS IN INDIA

(*In lakhs of rupees*)

Year	*Total of Great Britain's Public Investments at the End of the Year**	*Percentage of Private Investments to Public Investments†*	*Total of Great Britain's Private Investments at the End of the Year‡*	*Great Britain's Private Investments During the Year*
1897–98	30,987	27·0	8,367	—
1898–99	31,511	26·16	8,243	– 124
1899–00	31,898	25·39	8,099	– 144
1900–01	34,146	24·62	8,407	+ 308
1901–02	34,517	23·85	8,232	– 175
1902–03	35,300	23·08	8,147	– 85
1903–04	35,000	22·31	7,809	– 338
1904–05	35,550	21·54	7,658	– 151
1905–06	38,110	20·77	7,915	+ 257
1906–07	38,345	20·0	7,669	– 246
1907–08	39,989	18·5	7,398	– 271
1908–09	42,036	17·0	7,146	– 252
1909–10	44,433	15·5	6,887	– 259
1910–11	46,649	14·0	6,530	– 357
1911–12	47,251	13·5	6,379	– 151
1912–13	47,811	13·0	6,215	– 164
1913–14	48,279	12·5	6,035	– 180

* *Financial Statistics of British India*, vol. iii.

† Calculated according to the method explained in the preceding pages.

‡ For these calculations, see footnote on page 123.

years 1900–1 and 1905–6 were the only years during which there was a net excess of new private investments over withdrawals. As shown before, the total amount of British capital privately invested abroad showed an increase of Rs. 2,400 lakhs during the years 1897 to 1906. In the case of India there was a net reduction of Rs. 698 lakhs in that amount during the same period. This discrepancy, however, can be explained. The net increase of British private investments during 1897 to 1906 was due to the boom atmosphere generated by the era of large public investments which dawned in the year 1904. The period of heavy investments in India began in the year 1905–6, a year after "the recovery of British foreign investments." During this year there was a net excess of new private investments in India, but the excess was not big enough to counterbalance the total amount of net withdrawals which were effected during 1897 to 1904–5 due to political disturbances in India. Thus this net increase of British private investments was not transmitted to India, first because large public investments of British capital in India began a year later than they began in other countries, and, secondly, because the political disturbances in India during 1905–6 deterred the British investor from incurring fresh risks of private investments. The political unrest in India was also an important factor[1] which accentuated the general tendency of private investments to transform themselves into public investments or to be withdrawn from the country, especially from the year 1905–6 onwards.

Whether British private investments in India were completely withdrawn or returned to India as public investments, we consider the net amount of withdrawals every year as a debit item in India's International Balance of Accounts. If a part or the whole of the withdrawn capital was reinvested in India in public securities, it has already been accounted for

[1] C. K. Hobson, *The Export of Capital*, p. 158; E. Crammond, "British Investments Abroad," *Quarterly Review*, July 1907, p. 255.

as a credit item. We are counting it twice, once as a debit and once as a credit, because we do not know the actual amount of such capital.

The estimate of the total amount of foreign capital invested in India from 1898 to 1913 reached in this chapter is given in

TABLE XXIX

DIRECT AND INDIRECT ESTIMATES OF GREAT BRITAIN'S CAPITAL INVESTMENTS IN INDIA

(In lakhs of rupees)

	Direct Estimate			
Year	*Great Britain's Public Investments in India**	*Great Britain's Private Investments in India†*	*Total*	*Indirect Estimate‡*
1898–99	524	− 124	400	409
1899–00	387	− 144	243	1,225
1900–01	2,248	+ 308	2,556	1,308
1901–02	371	− 175	196	1,337
1902–03	783	− 85	698	577
1903–04	− 297	− 338	− 635	179
1904–05	547	− 151	396	1,190
1905–06	2,560	+ 257	2,817	2,497
1906–07	235	− 246	− 11	1,029
1907–08	1,644	− 271	1,373	2,668
1908–09	2,047	− 252	1,795	1,428
1909–10	2,397	− 259	2,138	2,465
1910–11	2,216	− 357	1,859	728
1911–12	602	− 151	451	565
1912–13	560	− 164	396	535
1913–14	468	− 180	288	1,831

* Supra, Table XXII. † Supra, Table XXVIII.
‡ Supra, Table XXI.

Table XXIX along with the corresponding indirect estimate reached in Chapter VI.

The indirect estimate of the total amount of foreign capital imported into India during the period of our study is greater by Rs. 5,011 lakhs than the corresponding figure disclosed by direct evidence. If the values of the various invisible items in our international transactions, calculated in the preceding chapters and the direct estimate of the total amount of foreign capital investments in India during 1898–1913 reached in this chapter are both approximately correct, these estimates should fairly agree with each other. The difference of Rs. 50 crores, which is not small, is therefore an indication of the fact that either the direct estimate or the data of the indirect estimate are defective. As the direct estimate of the British public investments in India is based upon fairly complete data, the discrepancy between the two estimates must be due largely to the calculations of the British private investments in India and the data of the indirect estimate. It is more likely that it can be located in the latter, which involves a large number of estimates.

In calculating the amount of interest charges paid by India we have already stated that the application of Lehfeldt's average rates of interest yielded by fixed-income colonial stocks to the Government borrowings after 1898 might exaggerate the volume of India's debits. This for the reason that the average rates of interest on fixed-income colonial stock are higher than the rates of interest at which Indian Government loans were being floated in London.[1] If the

[1]

Year	*Rate of Interest on India Government Loans** (*per cent*)	*Lehfeldt's Average Rate of Interest on Colonial Fixed Income Stock* (*per cent*)
1901	3·0	3·40
1902	3·0	3·21
1903	3·0	3·21
1904	3·0	3·78
1905	3·0	3·78
1906	3·0	3·85
1907	3·5	3·99
1908	3·5	4·04
1909	3·5	3·96
1910	3·5	4·19
1912	3·5	4·30
1913	4·0	4·44

* D. L. Dubey, *Indian Public Debt*, p. 31.

error that has crept into our calculation of interest payments by India due to this factor can be approximately determined and the necessary allowance made in the final balance of indebtedness, it will lessen the discrepancy between the direct and the indirect estimate of foreign capital invested in India. The *Financial Statistics of British India* give us all the details about the foreign borrowings of India on Government account and the interest payments thereon. By subtracting the figures of foreign borrowings on Government account from the indirect estimate of foreign capital investments in India reached in the last chapter, we shall get the annual amount of India's foreign borrowings on non-Government account. To the amount of interest charges paid by the Government every year, published in the *Financial Statistics*, we shall add the amount of interest charges payable on non-Government borrowings. To ascertain these interest charges the rate of interest charged on the total amount of such borrowings previous to 1898 will be assumed to be 3 per cent as before, and Lehfeldt's average rates of interest will be applied to the borrowings after 1898. The difference between the amount of annual interest payments arrived at by this process and that calculated in Chapter VI will represent the approximate error caused by the application of Lehfeldt's average rates of interest to India's foreign borrowings on Government account. Calculations made on the basis of this reasoning disclose an excess of about Rs. 300 lakhs in the figure of interest payments by India.

Then, again, in calculating the values of imports and exports we have not taken into account the sea-borne trade of non-British India. In a complete balance sheet of India's international payment, however, credit and debits arising out of that trade will have to be taken into account. Generally this sea-borne trade of non-British India reveals an excess of exports of about Rs. 130 lakhs every year.[1] This omission in

[1] See footnote on next page.

the primary data, therefore, explains an excess of Rs. 20 crores in the indirect estimate of foreign capital invested in India. As regards the extent of unliquidated liabilities the report of the Controller of Currency for 1913–14 bears ample evidence. Debits to the extent of Rs. 800 lakhs on account of heavy cotton imports at the close of that year remained to be unliquidated. The still unexplained difference of Rs. 19 crores between the two estimates may be due to the omission of trans-frontier trade and to errors arising out of the calculation of other invisible items. On the whole, considering the incomplete character of the data available for a direct estimate of the amount of foreign investments in India, the complicated character of the indirect estimate made in the preceding chapter and the necessary resort in both the cases to a large amount of guesswork, the agreement between the two estimates after these necessary corrections appears to be fairly close.

For individual years the two sets of estimates disclose much less agreement. The differences are especially great for the years 1899, 1900, 1901, 1906, 1907, 1910, and 1913. The excess of the indirect estimate of foreign capital imported into India in 1913–14 over the direct estimate may be due to the following causes. First, a large amount of credits due to India on account of the export of opium to China in previous years was probably received in 1913–14. Secondly, much larger sums than usual were due by India at the close of this year on account of the heavy imports of cotton goods the settlement of which was

Note to page 129.—In the year 1909–10 the figures were as follows:

	Imports *Rs.* 1,000	*Exports* *Rs.* 1,000
French Settlements	2,055	17,025
Portuguese Settlements	390	75
Travancore	1,140	810
Kathiawar	1,740	510
	5,325	18,420

postponed to the next year. There are also grounds for believing that the bank crisis which occurred during the year led to the Exchange banks strengthening their balances in India.[1] The rest of the discrepancies, as explained by J. Viner[2] in the case of Canada, may largely be due to the fact that the data used for both the estimates were much more comprehensive for the whole period of our study than for individual years, and the apportionment of the values of different items to individual years was based on conjectural hypotheses. But even if the data used were complete and accurate some discrepancy between the two sets of estimates for individual years might still be expected. A loan recorded in this chapter as made in a particular year may not have influenced the data used for the interest estimate in the same year. A public issue made in one year may represent the funding of an India Bill issue or a bank loan made some time previously, or the transformation of a private investment already made into a public investment. Imports may be financed by foreign borrowings either after or before the importation actually takes place. Other factors similar in character may cause large discrepancies between the direct and indirect estimates of foreign capital invested in India. However, the discrepancies between the two estimates for individual years due to such causes should offset each other in a series of years. The closeness of the two estimates for the whole period of our study corroborates the hypothesis that the margins between the estimates for individual years are largely the result of the difference in time between the flotation of a loan and its effect on the commodity balance of trade of the borrowing country.

[1] *Report of the Controller of Currency, 1913–14*, p. 53.
[2] J. Viner, *Canada's Balance of Indebtedness, 1900–13*, p. 140.

PART II

MECHANISM OF ADJUSTMENT

INTRODUCTORY

In the preceding part of this study we have ascertained the extent of India's deferred payments, i.e. her balance of international indebtedness during the period 1898 to 1913. These deferred payments are equivalent to her foreign borrowings. The pages that follow deal with the process by which India's balance of indebtedness adjusted itself to her foreign borrowings and brought about an equilibrium in the balance of immediate payments. As the foreign borrowings of the Government are spent almost entirely on the purchase of capital goods in England this problem of adjustment reduces itself practically to the adjustment of the private balance of indebtedness to India's non-Government borrowings.[1] Here, however, it is necessary to point out that the inflow of foreign capital was not the only factor—not even the main—disturbing the even balance between Indian credits and debits which existed in the years immediately preceding our period. The increasing volume and value of our commodity exports was another factor, more important than foreign borrowings, as we shall see later on, which upset that even balance. Hence, in trying to establish a causal relation between India's foreign borrowings and the substantive course of her foreign trade we should, where possible, make due allowance for other influences, including the unusually large demand for our export commodities, in the first decade and a half of the twentieth century. These other influences at times over-shadowed the effect of foreign borrowings.

If one and the same metal—gold or silver—is the circulating medium of the trading countries and moves freely between them, the mechanism of adjustment of the balance of inter-

[1] *Report on the Operations of the Currency Department, 1913–14*, p. 49.

national indebtedness of a country to its foreign borrowings will be, according to Mill, as follows:

> Commerce being supposed to be in a state of equilibrium when the obligatory remittances begin, the first remittance is necessarily made in money. This lowers prices in the remitting country, and raises them in the receiving. The natural effect is that more commodities are exported than before, and fewer imported, and that, on the score of commerce alone, a balance of money will be constantly due from the receiving to the paying country. When the debt thus annually due to the tributary country becomes equal to the annual tribute or other regular payment due from it, no further transmission of money takes place; the equilibrium of exports and imports will no longer exist but that of payments will; the exchange will be at par, the two debts will be set off against one another, and the tribute or remittance will be virtually paid in goods.

This explanation assumes, first, that the period of borrowings is immediately preceded by a period of even balance between the credits and debits of the borrowing country and, secondly, that the borrowings continue at an even and steady rate for a fairly long period.

Mill also states that the flow of the circulating medium, gold, from the lending country to the borrowing is preceded by the price of bills on the borrowing country, reaching the gold-export point in the lending country and remaining at it so long as the flow continues. Thus, when the circulating medium is the same in two or more trading countries and moves freely between them the mechanism of adjustment, according to Mill, consists of five successive stages in the following order:[2]

(i) A rise in the price of bills on the borrowing country to the gold-export point.

(ii) A flow of gold from the lending country to the borrowing

[1] J. S. Mill, *Principles of Political Economy*, Book iii, p. 627.

[2] J. Viner, *Canada's Balance of International Indebtedness, 1900–13*, p. 146.

country accompanied by foreign exchange at the gold-export and import points in the respective countries.

(iii) Adjustment of the price-levels between the two countries to the changes in the stock of monetary gold. Prices rising in the borrowing country and falling in the lending country.

(iv) Changes in imports and exports, the borrowing country acquiring an unfavourable balance of trade and the lending country acquiring a favourable balance of trade.

(v) After the unfavourable balance of trade of the borrowing country has become exactly equal to the rate of her foreign borrowings, the return of foreign exchange to parity, the cessation of specie flows and the stabilization of relative prices in the two countries at their new levels.

It is obvious, however, that the mechanism of the flow of specie, of prices, and wages rising or falling because of gold movement, of readjustment through a new level of prices and money incomes in each of the countries do not operate in the same way where the monetary systems rest on a different basis. If there is gold standard in one country and inconvertible paper in the other or gold in one and silver in the other, the mechanism of adjustment is somewhat different. However, it is a generally accepted theory that the ultimate phenomena of trade between two countries cannot be fundamentally different because of differences in their monetary systems.[1] Just as trade between individuals will be carried on in much the same fashion under barter as under money regime and on the same terms under one monetary system or another, so will be the trade between nations. But in precisely what manner are these results, ultimately similar as we expect them to be, brought about when the monetary systems are dissimilar? India during 1898 to 1913, the period of our study, had a gold-exchange standard. The even balance between her credits and debits was disturbed during this period, partly by her heavy borrowings in Great Britain, a country on the gold standard. The particular problem for us to investigate is the process by

[1] F. W. Taussig, *International Trade*, p. 337.

which the effects of this disturbing factor were absorbed by our balance of trade, and to what extent this process resembles the mechanism operating between two countries both on the gold standard. To this end we shall first consider in brief the essentials of the gold-exchange standard.

THE GOLD-EXCHANGE STANDARD

"Gold-exchange standard may be said to exist when gold does not circulate in a country to an appreciable extent, when the local currency is not necessarily redeemable in gold, but when the Government or Central Bank makes arrangements for the provision of foreign remittances in gold at a fixed maximum rate in terms of the local currency, the reserve necessary to provide these remittances being kept to a considerable extent abroad."[1] It seeks to maintain a fixed rate of exchange and to conduct international trade without the actual use of gold as currency, and with as little flow of gold from country to country as possible to settle their international balances of payment. (Though the local currency of a country adopting the gold-exchange standard is not necessarily convertible into gold, international trade is carried on as if it were so.)

The establishment of the gold-exchange standard in India was an accident.[2] The Fowler Committee, which reported in 1898, recommended a gold standard and a gold currency as the ideal to be realized by the Indian currency system in course of time. But by a turn of circumstances this ideal fell into the background, and the various changes that were intro-

[1] J. M. Keynes, *Indian Currency and Finance*, p. 30.

[2] *Report of the Royal Commission on Indian Finance and Currency, 1914*, paragraph 45: "The system actually in operation has accordingly never been deliberately adopted as a consistent whole, nor do the authorities themselves appear always to have had a clear idea of the final object to be attained. To a great extent this system is the result of a series of experiments."

duced into the Indian monetary system from time to time as measures to solve individual practical difficulties gave it the substance as well as the form of the gold-exchange standard system. The inauguration of the system as well as the formation of its "central mechanism," the Gold Standard Reserve, dates from Sir Edward Law's minute of June 28, 1900. However, for all practical purposes, and for the sake of this study, the system can be said to have existed in India from 1898, the year in which the Fowler Committee reported. The main features of the gold-exchange standard system as it existed in India during the pre-war period may now be summarized as follows:

(i) The rupee, a silver token coin, was unlimited legal tender and was not convertible by law.

(ii) The British sovereign was unlimited legal tender at £1 to Rs. 15 and was convertible at that rate, i.e. the Government was bound to give Rs. 15 in exchange for £1.

(iii) The Government, as a matter of administrative practice, were willing to give sovereigns for rupees, but that entirely depended on their discretion, and large quantities of gold could not be obtained by tendering rupees.

(iv) Similarly, as a matter of administrative practice the Government were willing to sell sterling bills on London in return for rupees at a rate not more unfavourable than 1s. $3\frac{29}{32}$d. per rupee. For this a gold reserve was formed and kept in London.

(v) To prevent the flow of gold to India the Secretary of State for India had put a standing notification that he would sell Council Bills on India at 1s. $4\frac{1}{8}$d. the gold-import point of India.

To explain the mechanism of adjustment of India's balance of indebtedness to her foreign borrowings under the gold-exchange standard we now take up for examination the operation of exchange variations, gold movements, changes in relative price-levels, and changes in the commodity balance of trade in the order given. The influences of these factors will be considered mainly from the Indian point of view.

CHAPTER VI

FOREIGN EXCHANGE AND GOLD MOVEMENTS

(1) FOREIGN EXCHANGE

VARIATIONS in the rate of foreign exchange through their influence on the profitability or otherwise of commodity imports and exports and on the transfer of securities and bank deposits from country to country bring about an adjustment of international balances. If the supply of bills on foreign countries is larger than the demand for them, they fall in price and the currencies of the foreign countries depreciate in terms of the currency of the country in question. Consequently, foreign goods become cheaper by the amount of depreciation of their currency units. Imports of foreign goods increase. On the other hand, if the supply of bills is less than the demand for them, they rise in price and the currencies of the foreign countries go to a premium. This makes foreign goods dearer by the amounts of the premia and their exports are checked. When India begins to borrow in London, the supply of bills on London outstrips the demand, and the sterling exchange becomes favourable to her. The favourable exchange gives a bounty to importers and imports are stimulated, while the same favourable exchange becomes a tax on exporters and exports from India are checked. In this fashion at least a small portion of the borrowed funds comes to be transferred to India in the form of commodities. However, to understand the exact significance of the part played by the variations in the exchange rate in the mechanism of adjustment we must distinguish between casual and permanent disturbances to the even balance of credits and debits.

In the absence of speculative purchases and sales of foreign exchange, the exchange rate would always stand at one of three positions. If there is an even balance between the immediate receipts and payments of a country, the exchange will be at par; if the balance is against the country the exchange will be at the gold-export point, and if the balance is favourable, the exchange will be at the gold-import point. But, in fact, the exchange is always fluctuating between the gold-points and is rarely at par. The variations between the gold-points are due to the calculations and trading of the bankers and brokers who deal in foreign exchange. They sell forward at less than the gold-export point when the balance of payments is turning against the country and when they believe that the current of payments will turn round in due time. They buy exchange in advance at more than the gold-import point if they believe it can be done with profit in anticipation of a subsequent movement in the opposite direction. The general effect of these operations is that they prevent the exchange rate from reaching the gold-points and thereby prevent gold movements between the trading countries. However, the exchange rate can be prevented from reaching the gold-points only when the fluctuations in the international balance of indebtedness about the even balance of credits and debits are temporary. So long as the basic conditions tend to bring about an even balance of payments, casual disturbances in one direction are likely to be offset after a time by disturbances in the reverse direction. In fact, the operations of Exchange dealers and speculators are based on this assumption. It can, therefore, be conceded that so long as the disturbances to the even balance of credits and debits of a country are casual and tend to be offset by disturbances in the opposite direction within a short time, variations in exchange rate between gold-points are an important factor in the adjustment of the balance of indebtedness. Even then they bring about the adjustment not so much by their effect on the imports and exports of commodities as through their influence on the transfer of securities and bank balances, on the settlement or postponement of maturing obligations, and on international short-term loans.

Apart from casual disturbances, the even balance between the credits and debits of a country is likely to be upset by other factors, more or less permanent. A growing demand for a country's exportable commodities or continued foreign borrowings are instances of such factors. The adjustment of the balance of international indebtedness to foreign borrowings consists not in the re-establishment of the equilibrium between all credits and all debits immediate as well as deferred, but in the establishment of an even balance between immediate payments through the creation of an excess of trade debits over trade credits equal to the amount of current foreign borrowings so that the borrowed capital enters the country in the form of commodities and not of gold. If foreign capital continues to be imported for a fairly long period at a steady rate, the change in the exchange rate alone will not be able to bring about these adjustments without being indefinitely favourable to the borrowing country. But the exchange rates cannot continue to be favourable to any country having a gold standard, or even for the matter of that a gold-exchange standard, without reaching the gold-import point and giving rise to an inflow of gold or its equivalents.

The exchange rates show an aversion to reaching the gold-points only when the disturbances to the even balance of payments are temporary and when there is the probability that the turn of the exchanges in one direction will soon be followed by a turn in the other direction. They are prevented from reaching the gold-points in consequence of minor disturbances to the balance of payments by means of financial operations—such as postponement or settlement of maturing obligations, transfer of securities and bank deposits, investments in short-term loans—which either create payments in one direction or diminish the volume of payments in the other direction. Such operations are, however, necessarily limited in their volume and are undertaken as temporary measures to be reversed in their direction, when the balance of payments moves to the other side of the equilibrium. If the balance of immediate payments, even for a short time, is such that the supply of or demand for foreign bills is greatly in excess of the demand or supply, the additional demand or supply created by the financial operations in the speculative market will not be sufficient to keep the exchange within gold-points. Much more so if the supply of foreign bills continues to be greatly in excess of the demand for a pretty long period, as generally happens in the case of continued foreign borrowings. Financial operations which are attractive to the speculators so long as disturbances are temporary cease to be so when the disturbing factor is more or less permanent.

Gold movements play their part in the mechanism of adjustment through their effect on the prices of commodities entering into international trade. Therefore, though a favourable exchange rate may be expected to co-operate with the effect of gold movements on prices at the beginning of foreign borrowings to stimulate commodity imports and check exports, variations in the exchanges exhaust their direct influence, when a fall in the foreign exchange is first a preliminary to the import of gold and then accompanies the import of gold.[1] When prices in the lending and the borrowing country

[1] Professor J. H. Hollander contends that the adjustment of the balance of indebtedness to foreign borrowings is effected without gold movements, through the influence of exchange variations within the gold-points on the commodity balance of trade. "International Trade Under Depreciated Paper: A Criticism." 32. *Quarterly Journal of Economics*, p. 678.

Professor Taussig in a rejoinder to Hollander shows that he is over-estimating the influence of the variations in the exchange rate in affecting the substantive course of trade. Ibid., p. 692.

J. Viner goes further and gives a satisfactory demonstration by his study of Canadian conditions during 1900 to 1913 that "exchange rates cannot operate at all, except at the beginning of the period of borrowings." *Canada's Balance of International Indebtedness, 1900–13*, p. 151.

stabilize at the new levels, the balance of immediate payments becomes even, gold imports cease, and exchange returns to parity.

RUPEE-STERLING EXCHANGE AND THE GOLD-POINTS

India's foreign trade is financed by Exchange Banks which have their head offices in London. The Indian branches of these banks discount the bills drawn by the Indian exporters and send them for collection to their head offices in London. The Indian exporters receive their payments in rupees while the Exchange Banks in London collect the bills in sterling. To reimburse themselves with rupee funds in India again to finance the export trade the Exchange Banks purchase as many private bills on India as can be obtained. But generally the supply of bills on India, thanks to her favourable commodity balance of trade, is less than the demand for them. Under the circumstances the rupee sterling exchange should rise to the gold-import point and the favourable balance of trade be settled by gold imports. But this process could not operate during the period of our study because of the intervention of an extraneous influence. The Secretary of State for India who had annually to make payments in sterling for "Home Charges," etc., taking advantage of the normal favourable balance of trade, offered to sell bills on India. The "Council Bills," as these bills were called, found ready purchasers in the Exchange Banks and were cashed at Bombay, Calcutta, or Madras from the Government Treasuries, where the Home Charges which were chargeable to the Indian revenue were collected in rupees. Since 1904 the Secretary of State had been selling the Council Bills, not only to defray the Home Charges, but also to meet the demands of the Exchange Banks for remittances to India on trade account. By the sale of Council Bills the Government of India saved the expenses of remitting rupees to London to purchase gold for the liquidation of her sterling obligations, while the

Secretary of State gained an extra commission for dealing in rupee exchange. Thus, as the Secretary of State for India was one of the largest dealers in rupee exchange, the price at which Council Bills were bought and sold can well be considered an index of the rupee-sterling exchange.

The Fowler Committee fixed the value of the rupee at 1s. 4d. by making the sovereign a legal tender coin exchangeable for 15 rupees. The maintenance of this ratio was the main object of the Government's currency policy during the pre-war period of the gold-exchange standard. The range of variations in the rupee-sterling exchange or the gold-points were therefore determined by the cost of remitting sovereigns from London to Calcutta or from Calcutta to London. This cost of remitting gold from London to India generally did not exceed $\frac{1}{8}$d. per rupee. The upper limit to which the rupee-sterling exchange could fluctuate was therefore 1s. $4\frac{1}{8}$d., while the lower limit was 1s. $3\frac{29}{32}$d. These, however, are the extreme limits between which the rupee-sterling exchange could fluctuate. Actually the cost of importing gold into India depended on complex causes varying considerably from time to time and might have been less than $\frac{1}{8}$d. per rupee with consequent reduction in the gold-import point.[1]

The cost of remitting gold from London to Calcutta consists of freight, insurance charges, and loss of interest during transit. Variations in freight and insurance charges are comparatively unimportant. "The main part of variation in the gold-point arises either out of the possibility of getting sovereigns from other sources—than England—or from variations in the rate of interest."[2] These other sources during 1898–99 to 1913–14 were the sovereigns in transit from Australia or the

[1] The Government had practically pledged their word to do all in their power to prevent the depreciation of the gold value of the rupee below 1s. $3\frac{29}{32}$d. Vide H. Stanley Jevons, *Money, Banking and Exchange in India*, 1922.

[2] J. M. Keynes, *Indian Currency and Finance*, p. 115.

sovereigns ready to be exported from Egypt. Whenever the Australian exchange was such that it paid to export sovereigns from Australia to London, it was always profitable for the banks which exported them to get cash in London for their delivery in India. For while the freight and insurance charges on the shipment of sovereigns to London and to India, which lies on the shipping route between Australia and London, were the same, the bank could get its money a fortnight earlier by delivering the sovereigns in India rather than carrying them straight to London. This meant a gain of a fortnight's interest on the money. It was, therefore, willing to accept about 1s. $3\frac{31}{32}$d. in London for 1s. 4d. delivered in India—$\frac{1}{32}$ being the interest on 1s. 4d. for a fortnight at 5 per cent per annum. The gold purchased in this fashion became equivalent to a telegraphic transfer on India, i.e. it was worth $\frac{1}{32}$d. more than the Councils. Hence, whenever the price of Council Bills was more than 1s. $3\frac{15}{16}$d. per rupee, sovereigns in transit from Australia were preferred as a means of remittance to India.

The gold exports from Egypt were not so serious a competitor to Council Bills as the Australian sovereigns. As the cost of sending gold to India from Egypt, which lies between India and London, is the same as the cost of sending gold to London, an Egyptian bank remitting gold could accept anything more than 1s. 4d. in London for the delivery in India of a rupee worth of gold. Hence, whenever the Alexandrian exchange on London was below par and the Council Bills were at about 1s. $4\frac{1}{16}$d. per rupee, Egyptian gold could undercut the Councils as a means of remittance to India. However, the amount of remittances available from this source was very limited because the weak Alexandrian exchange which stimulated the flow of gold out of Egypt gathered strength when some gold was exported and thus modified the conditions governing the gold flow. Nevertheless, when at the end of the season the Egyptian banks found themselves in possession of more gold than they needed, the Councils had to be sold at a relatively low price to prevent the flow of that gold to India.

Besides the availability of gold from Australia and Egypt for exportation to India the variations in the Indian bank-rate also led to variations in the gold-import point. As said before, the loss caused to the exporters of gold from London is $\frac{1}{32}$d. per rupee when the Indian bank-rate is at 5 per cent. If this bank-rate rises the loss will be more; if it falls the loss will be less with consequent changes in the gold-import point.

These considerations lead us to the conclusion that the gold-import point of India during the pre-war period of the gold-exchange standard was subject to variations from extraneous causes like a fall in the Australian or Alexandrian exchange. To the extent the variations in the rupee-sterling exchange about par were due to these causes, they were not determined by India's balance of immediate payments. To carry out his policy, which was to prevent export of more gold to India than was actually required for absorption by the public,[1] the Secretary of State had to offer Council Bills at a price at which the Australian or the Egyptian gold might have been delivered in India. But it is not always easy to know at exactly what price Australian or Egyptian gold will undercut Council Bills as a means of remittance, and hence "not infrequently" they were "unintentionally sold at a price which made it cheaper to send gold." If we leave out of consideration these extraneous factors which were never very serious, the gold-import point of India during the pre-war period of the gold-exchange standard could be regarded as being 1s. $4\frac{1}{8}$d. (1s. 4·125d.) and the gold-export point at 1s. $3\frac{29}{32}$d. (1s. 3·906d.), below which the Secretary of State did not offer any bills.

To understand the part played by variations in the exchange rate in bringing about an adjustment between India's balance of indebtedness and her foreign borrowings we give in Table XXX the average rate of exchange, the commodity

[1] G. F. Shirras, *Indian Finance and Banking*, p. 304.

balance of trade, and the foreign borrowings for every year during 1898 to 1913.

Throughout the greater part of the period of our study

TABLE XXX

THE AVERAGE RATE OF EXCHANGE, THE COMMODITY BALANCE OF TRADE, AND FOREIGN BORROWINGS

Year	*Average Rate of Exchange* *s. d.*	*Balance of Trade* *Rs.* 1,00,000	*Foreign Borrowings. Indirect Estimate** *Rs.* 1,00,000
1898–99	1 3·972	3,556	409
1899–00	1 4·069	2,700	1,225
1900–01	1 3·973	2,291	1,308
1901–02	1 3·988	3,486	1,337
1902–03	1 4·002	3,575	577
1903–04	1 4·047	4,534	179
1904–05	1 4·045	3,854	1,190
1905–06	1 4·042	3,283	2,497
1906–07	1 4·087	2,762	1,029
1907–08	1 4·031	1,176	2,668
1908–09	1 3·931	1,732	1,428
1909–10	1 4·037	4,220	2,465
1910–11	1 4·060	5,141	728
1911–12	1 4·083	5,067	565
1912–13	1 4·059	4,144	535
1913–14	1 4·069	3,596	1,831

* The indirect estimate has been preferred to the direct estimate because it gives the figures of capital actually imported in India every year during the period. The direct estimate is based on the years of flotation. But the capital floated in a particular year is not necessarily imported in the same year. To trace the relation between foreign exchange and foreign borrowings we want the estimate based on the years of importation.

sterling funds were at a discount in India, this being due to the increasing demand for India's exports and her foreign borrowings, the two factors which disturbed the even balance between India's credits and debits. It is not, however, possible to trace the variations in the exchange due to either of the factors severally.

As seen in the table the average rate of exchange was below par only during four years: 1898–99, 1900–1, 1901–2, and 1908–9. The unfavourable average rate of exchange in the year 1898–99 was due to the fact that the sterling value of the rupee, which had been rising since 1895 as a result of the closure of mints to the free coinage of silver, had not yet reached 1s. 4d. till the middle of that year. It can even be said that this improvement in the sterling value of the rupee was brought about by the favourable balance of trade of the year. In 1900–1 it was the decrease in the favourable balance of trade which brought about a fall in the exchange rate. The slight improvement in the exchange rate, still below par, during the next year, in spite of heavy foreign borrowings and a large favourable balance of trade is apparently anomalous. However, it ceases to be so when we know that the marked revival in the favourable balance of trade came late in the year,[1] and thus had no proportionate effect on the average of the rates of exchange prevailing during the whole year. It can, therefore, be legitimately inferred that simultaneously with the increase in the favourable balance of trade and foreign borrowings there was an improvement in the exchange rate. The circumstances of the year 1908–9 were exceptional. The American crisis of 1907 overtook India in the fiscal year 1908–9 in the form of an unfavourable balance of payments and an unfavourable exchange caused by a fall in the volume of Indian exports and her foreign borrowings. The decrease in the volume of foreign borrowings as compared with the preceding year was as important a factor in turning the exchange rate as the smaller volume of exports.[2]

Excluding these four years the rate of exchange was favourable to India throughout the period 1898 to 1913. It was the result both of an increasingly favourable balance of

[1] W. L. Thorp, *Business Annals*, p. 335.

[2] J. M. Keynes, "Recent Economic Events in India," 19. *Economic Journal*, p. 61.

trade caused by the growing volume of exports every year and the foreign borrowings which, however, were fluctuating in their volume. It is not possible to ascertain the effect of these factors separately.

The range of variations between the fortnightly averages[1] of the rates of exchange as well as the annual averages was very narrow. Even the maximum range to which the exchange rate could have fluctuated, i.e. the difference between the gold-points, was about 2 per cent. Evidently the fluctuations in the exchange rate cannot be supposed to have exerted any appreciable influence on the relative volume of Indian imports and exports in bringing about the adjustment of her balance of indebtedness to her foreign borrowings.

(2) GOLD MOVEMENTS

As we have said before, variations in the exchange rate play an important part in bringing about the adjustment of the even balance of international credits and debits to casual disturbances. But in adjusting them to major and continuous disturbances, caused, for example, by an increasing demand for the export commodities of a country or by an influx of foreign capital, their influence is very small. The adjustment is necessarily effected in the case of countries on the gold standard by gold movements operating directly on the balance of payments and, more important, indirectly through their effect on the prices of international commodities[2] and, consequently, on the commodity balance of trade.

The even balance between India's international credits and debits was disturbed in the beginning of the pre-war period of the gold-exchange standard by two factors of great importance. One was the increasing demand for her exports,

[1] "Statistics of British India," vol. iii, *Financial Statistics*, pp. 92–95.

[2] "International commodities" are the commodities which enter into international trade as opposed to the "domestic commodities," which do not move between one country and another.

and the other the import of British capital. Both these factors were operating during the major part of the period of our study. The variations in the rupee-sterling exchange between 1s. $4\frac{1}{8}$d. the gold-import point and 1s. $3\frac{29}{32}$d. the gold-export point, even if they had been of the maximum extent, could not have been a sufficiently powerful factor to adjust India's balance of payments to the influence of either of these two factors. In fact, the variations in the annual and fortnightly averages of the rates of exchange were, as stated before, very small. Therefore the adjustment of the balance of payments could have been brought about in the main—almost wholly—by means of gold imports through their effects—direct and indirect—on the Indian price-level. But generally the gold which India imports in settlement of her favourable balance of payments is not used on an extensive scale for internal circulation, nor is it kept in bank reserves and mobilized for credit and exchange purposes. "It is used for conversion into ornaments and for similar purposes; it is also hoarded."[1] Even sovereigns and half-sovereigns which were declared legal tender in India in 1898 did not form an appreciable portion of the currency circulation in India during the pre-war period of the gold-exchange standard.[2] All the imports of gold during the period of our study cannot, therefore, be supposed to have affected the Indian price-level. Only that portion of the gold-imports which either went directly into circulation in the form of sovereigns or indirectly through Government Treasuries and the paper currency reserves in the form of silver rupees and notes—the chief circulating media of exchange in India—could have affected prices.

[1] G. Findlay Shirras, *Indian Finance and Banking*, p. 280.

[2] The attempt to introduce sovereigns in circulation made in 1900–1 failed. But it is reported that sovereigns were being used as currency in some of the provinces of India in the closing years of our period. Nevertheless their proportion to the total currency circulation in India was insignificant. See H. F. Howard, *India and the Gold Standard*, pp. 28 and 47.

Since the closure of mints to the free coinage of silver in India the only way of making additions to the currency circulation was to tender gold to the Government in exchange for rupees or notes. The volume of paper currency issued on the backing of Government securities was an insignificant percentage of the total currency circulation. In 1892 the value of the currency notes backed by Government securities was Rs. 8,00 lakhs. It increased to Rs. 1,000 lakhs in 1897 to Rs. 1,200 in 1905, and to Rs. 1,400 lakhs in 1911.[1] To get rupees in India it was left to the option of those possessing gold and requiring rupees in exchange to tender it either to the Government in India or to the Secretary of State for India in London. The Council Bills in effect were in the nature of certificates, stating that the holder of such bills had deposited a certain amount of gold with the Secretary of State. The Government of India were bound to cash these certificates on their presentation to the Treasury. Since the introduction of the gold-exchange standard in India the Council Bills had been used by the Secretary of State to prevent the flow to India of that portion of our gold imports which represented a demand for additional currency. This he effected by offering Council Bills at rates below the gold-import point. Thus the gold which was imported into India, in spite of the Secretary of State's offer of Council Bills, must have been mostly for industrial uses or for the purposes of hoarding. It had, therefore, no more effect on the price-level in the country than the import of any other commodity.

As the prevention of monetary gold[2] flowing to India was

[1] Though the securities backing the paper currency in India were chiefly to be the Government of India rupee securities, it was decided in 1905 that Rs. 200 lakhs and in 1911 Rs. 400 lakhs may be in the form of English securities.

[2] By the term "monetary gold" we mean the gold which influenced the Indian price-level as distinct from the non-monetary gold which had no more effect on the Indian price-level than the importation of any other commodity.

the declared policy of the Secretary of State, and since it was carried out by offering Council Bills at rates lower than the gold-import point, the amount of Council Bills sold every year can be considered to represent approximately the amount of monetary gold which could have been imported in India in the absence of the mechanism of Council Bills.[1] In fact, even though this gold was prevented from flowing to India, the price-level in the country was affected in the same way as if it actually flowed. That is to say, the gold which was intercepted by the Secretary of State in London had its full effect on the currency circulation in India through the encashment of Council Bills in India. To trace how far India's heavy surplus of commodity exports and her foreign borrowings entered the country in the form of monetary gold, i.e. in the form of Council Bills, we give in Table XXXI the relevant figures.

The sale of Council Bills as explained above is the equivalent of the flow of monetary gold to India that would have other-

[1] All the Council Bills cashed in India do not represent a net addition to the currency circulation. As explained in Chapter V the main function of the mechanism of Council Bills is to enable the Secretary of State to meet the sterling liabilities of the Government of India on account of the Home Charges. In order to meet these liabilities the Government of India collect rupees by means of taxation. When people pay the taxes for remission to a foreign country the currency circulation in the remitting country is reduced to that extent. But in India the rupees collected for remission to England are again returned into circulation in payment of the Council Bills drawn by the Secretary of State. He gets from the Exchange Banks the gold he wants to meet his sterling liabilities while the Exchange Banks in return get the rupees they need in India. The Council Bills which the banks purchase from the Secretary of State are paid by means of the rupees collected for remission to England and to that extent there is no addition to the currency circulation. It can therefore be said that the net addition to the currency circulation caused by the encashment of Council Bills will be equal to the total sale of Council Bills by the Secretary of State minus the taxes on account of Home Charges collected by the Government of India.

wise taken place. The function of the movements of monetary gold is to settle the unliquidated balances of payments in respect of commodities (including the non-monetary gold) and services. India's balance of trade is generally favourable to her because of her peculiarly strong position in regard to the

TABLE XXXI

COMMODITY BALANCE OF TRADE, FOREIGN BORROWINGS, AND THE SALE OF COUNCIL BILLS

(In lakhs of rupees)

Year	*Commodity Balance of Trade*	*Foreign Borrowings*	*Council Bills Sold by the Secretary of State**
1898–99	3,556	409	2,808
1899–00	2,700	1,225	2,848
1900–01	2,291	1,308	1,998
1901–02	3,486	1,337	2,783
1902–03	3,575	577	2,775
1903–04	4,534	179	3,568
1904–05	3,854	1,190	3,654
1905–06	3,283	2,497	4,722
1906–07	2,762	1,029	4,989
1907–08	1,176	2,668	2,292
1908–09	1,732	1,428	2,096
1909–10	4,220	2,465	4,102
1910–11	5,141	728	3,955
1911–12	5,067	565	4,037
1912–13	4,144	535	3,850
1913–14	3,596	1,831	4,660

* *Statistical Abstract for British India.*

export trade.[1] But, especially during the period 1898 to 1913, this normal feature of Indian trade became prominent. First, because since the beginning of the present century the foreign demands for India's export commodities, which are mostly raw materials and foodstuffs, increased rapidly as a result of

[1] Cf. W. L. Thorp, *Business Annals*, p. 332.

"With the exception of the years 1856–62 and a short period since the close of the war, Indian foreign trade has recorded a large excess of exports over imports."

the rapid industrial development in the West. Secondly, because India was importing large amounts of foreign capital during the period. As both these factors were working simultaneously it is not possible to ascertain exactly how much of the foreign borrowings of India were transferred to this country in the form of Council Bills. The increased volume of our foreign imports, along with the increase in our foreign exports and foreign borrowings, suggests that some part of the new capital raised abroad must have entered the country in the form of goods, but the heavy sales of Council Bills show that a large part of it must have come in the form of money. The inference drawn by J. M. Keynes from an analytical study of India's foreign trade during 1900 to 1908 can be cited in support of our statement. He says: "At the earlier stage imports, though steadily progressing in value, did not leap forward so rapidly, with the result that a larger balance of trade remained to be met by the sale of Council Bills. The new wave of prosperity seems not unnaturally to have required and attracted foreign loanable capital in a more ample stream than during the years immediately preceding it, and this circumstance, combining with a large excess of exports over private imports, swelled the sale of Council Bills to an unprecedented extent, the influx of new capital being, on the whole, the more important factor of the two."[1] This statement of Keynes seems to be a little exaggerated, nevertheless, it does indicate that the demand for Council Bills was at least partially caused by India's foreign borrowings.

SUMMARY

The conclusions of this chapter can be summarized as follows:

First, as the two disturbing factors—the increased foreign demand for India's exportable commodities and her foreign

[1] J. M. Keynes, "Recent Economic Events in India," 19. *Economic Journal*, 1909.

borrowings—were working simultaneously, the process of adjustment to their individual influence could not be traced separately.

Secondly, adjustment to both these disturbing factors was brought about in the same way. The rupee-sterling exchange was favourable to India during the major part of the period under consideration, and the sale of Council Bills, which played the part of gold movements in India, was very large throughout the period, except on one or two occasions.

Thirdly, in keeping the rupee-sterling exchange favourable to India and in creating a large demand for Council Bills to settle her balance of payments, foreign borrowings had some influence along with the increased commodity exports.

CHAPTER VII

CHANGES IN RELATIVE PRICE-LEVELS AND THE ADJUSTMENT OF THE BALANCE OF PAYMENT

In gold-standard countries the readjustment of the balance of payments disturbed by more or less permanent factors like an increase in the foreign demand for exports or in the amount of foreign borrowings is brought about by means of gold movements and changes in relative price-levels, which in their turn influence the commodity balance of trade. The importation of gold under the gold standard involves a change in the incomes "spendable" by the people of the countries concerned. For example, if the people of A borrow an additional X million rupees from the people of B, the former have X million more to spend and the latter X million less. Having more to spend altogether, the demand of the people in A for foreign goods as well as for the goods produced in their own country increases, while the reverse happens in B where people have now less to spend. The increase in the effective demand of A for goods in general, foreign and domestic, raises its price-level, while, on the other hand, the fall in the effective demand of B lowers its price-level.[1] If the volume of foreign borrowings of A remains constant for a long period, the relative changes in the "spendable incomes" and consequently in the price-levels in the borrowing and the lending countries bring about an excess of commodity imports into A from B equal to the amount of A's foreign borrowings, and further gold movements from B to A are stopped. The favourable balance of payments caused by the increase in foreign borrowings is in the beginning settled by an inflow of gold, but ultimately by a change in the commodity balance of trade. Similar will be the case if the favourable balance of payments is caused by

[1] Barrett Whale, *International Trade*, p. 78.

an increase in the foreign demand for A's exportable commodities.[1]

Under the gold-exchange standard as it prevailed in India during the pre-war period, the immediate settlement of her large favourable balances of payment caused by both the factors mentioned above working simultaneously, was brought about mainly by the sale of Council Bills. In the transmission of "spendable income" to India these bills played the same part which gold imports would have played had India been on the gold standard. Naturally, we should expect an increase in the spendable income of India due to her increased foreign borrowings and the increasing foreign demand for her exportable commodities during the period of our study to force up the price-level. At the same time, because India's capital imports during the period under consideration were almost wholly from the United Kingdom, we should expect the prices there to display a falling tendency. However, it is noteworthy in this connection that there was a world-wide rise in prices between 1897 and 1914, due to a general business prosperity, which was only punctuated by the crisis of 1907.[2] Therefore, what we should expect (according to the theory of

[1] The process of readjustment is similar in the two cases. But the final results are not the same. In the case of foreign borrowings as well as of increased demand for exports, the preliminary gap between "incomes" and payments is ultimately restored by an expansion of imports. But in the case of foreign borrowings the margin may be filled up in part by a contraction of exports, which is, of course, by hypothesis impossible in the other case. Again, in the case of foreign borrowings the commodity balance of trade is never restored, but this happens in the case of increased demand for exports.

[2] W. C. Mitchell, *Business Cycles*, p. 78. Also compare W. T. Layton, *An Introduction to the Study of Prices*, p. 83. "The features of the price curve since the last upward movement began are the booms of 1900 and 1907 with a considerable depression in the intervening years, and since 1907 a drop with a further rise to the highest point in 1913. Thus there are two fairly long cycles and a short one which has probably not yet reached its climax. But whether one looks to the maximum points or to the bottom points of these three cycles, there is shown an equally steady upward movement."

relative price-levels as a factor in the mechanism of adjustment) is not a rise of prices in India and a fall of prices in Great Britain, but a relatively greater rise in India than in Great Britain.

INDEX NUMBERS OF INDIAN PRICES

An index number of prices is a measure of the composite effect of the numerous forces which cause prices of individual commodities to rise or fall. There are four Index Numbers of wholesale prices in India available for the period of our study:

(i) Atkinson's Index Number.
(ii) The Official Index Number prepared by the Department of Statistics, Government of India.
(iii) The Indices prepared by the Prices Enquiry Committee.

Atkinson's Index Number is calculated from 111 prices of 48 commodities; 60 prices representing articles of food, 29 prices representing raw materials, 11 prices representing manufactures, and 11 prices representing imported articles.[1] The weights are assigned according to the production and imports of the selected articles during the year 1893. The Index Number was published by its author in the *Journal of the Royal Statistical Society*, September 1909, and has since then been compiled by the Department of Statistics on the same lines. The main criticism of Atkinson's Index Number is that it does not use variable weights. However, as a rough indication of the trend of prices in India during the pre-war years of the twentieth century, it may be accepted as more reliable than any other unweighted Index Number.

The Official Index Number is compiled from the price quotations of 39 staple commodities, 11 imported and 28 exported, and the base year selected in 1873. The articles are

[1] F. J. Atkinson, "Rupee Prices in India, 1870 to 1908," 72. *Journal of the Royal Statistical Society*, p. 497.

selected according to their domestic importance rather than their prominence in the foreign trade of India. The "articles of export" include 9 foodstuffs, 15 raw materials, and 4 manufactured articles. The greatest drawback of this Index Number is that it assigns equal weights to all the commodities it includes.

The Prices Enquiry Committee has selected "as many as possible of the main staple articles of Indian production and consumption" for the preparation of their Index Numbers. In all, the number of articles with their varieties counted separately comes up to 140. They have been classified as (i) cereals; (ii) pulses; peas or split peas; (iii) sugars; (iv) tea and coffee; (v) other articles of food, (*a*) condiments and spices, (*b*) animals and animal produce, (*c*) others; (vi) oil seeds, oils and oil cakes; (vii) textile jute; (viii) textile cotton; (ix) other textiles; (x) hides and skins; (xi) metals; (xii) other raw and manufactured articles; (xiii) building materials.[1] The Committee prepared two Indices, one Weighted and the other Unweighted, with the quinquennium 1890–4 as the base period. The weights assigned to the commodities in the Weighted Index Number are calculated for every quinquennium since 1890.

In general, statisticians support the use of Weighted in preference to Unweighted Index Numbers as measures of the general trend of prices, if the weights used are not wholly arbitrary but related even though very roughly to the relative importance of the commodities included in the Index.[2] Accordingly, Atkinson's Index and the Weighted Index of the Prices Enquiry Committee are preferable to the Official Index and the Unweighted Index of the Prices Enquiry Committee. Again, between these two a choice has to be made. The weights of Atkinson's Index Number are based on the importance of the commodities selected by him, in a par-

[1] *Report on the Enquiry into the Rise of Prices in India*, vol. i, p. 71.

[2] J. Viner, *Canada's Balance of International Indebtedness, 1900–13*, p. 224.

ticular year, viz. 1893. Under the rapidly changing conditions of production and trade which characterized the pre-war period of the gold-exchange standard in India the importance and, consequently, the weights of her different staple commodities cannot be expected to remain unaltered over a long period. In fact, the weights of commodities like rice, sugar, indigo, and coal did change considerably during the period 1893 to 1913.[1] Hence, the Weighted Index Number of the Prices Enquiry Committee which uses varying weights would be more satisfactory than Atkinson's Index Number which uses constant weights. For the sake of this study we shall, therefore, use Atkinson's Index Number and the Weighted Index Number of the Prices Enquiry Committee, but predominantly the latter in preference to all the other Indices of wholesale prices in India.

INDEX NUMBERS OF WHOLESALE PRICES IN THE UNITED KINGDOM

For the United Kingdom the Official Index Number of the Labour Department, Board of Trade, and Sauerbeck's Index Number would be used. Here, however, it is necessary to bear in mind that both these indices as well as the Index Number of the *Economist* are constructed mainly from the price quotations of raw materials and foodstuffs which are largely import commodities in that country.[2] In a creditor country during a period of increasing foreign lending, such as was the period 1898–99 to 1913–14 for the United Kingdom, import prices should rise relatively to domestic and export prices.[3] Moreover, after 1900 the rise in prices all over the

[1] C. N. Vakil and Muranjan, *Currency and Prices in India*, pp. 306, 307.

[2] Cf. A. W. Flux, "Measurement of Price Changes," 74. *Journal of the Royal Statistical Society*, p. 169. "Of the 47 price series used in constructing the British Board of Trade Price Index 35 are not only for import commodities but are the average import values."

[3] C. K. Hobson, *The Export of Capital*, p. 219.

DATA OF CHART I

INDICES OF WHOLESALE PRICES FOR INDIA AND UNITED KINGDOM

Year	*India—Atkinson's Index**	*India—Prices Enquiry Committee†*	*United Kingdom Labour Department Board of Trade.‡*	*United Kingdom Sauerbeck.§*
1898–99	100	100	100	100
1899–00	97	100	99	106
1900–01	114	112	108	117
1901–02	111	110	104	110
1902–03	102	106	104	109
1903–04	99	105	108	109
1904–05	96	106	106	110
1905–06	108	113	106	113
1906–07	127	128	109	120
1907–08	134	133	114	126
1908–09	143	132	111	114
1909–10	129	122	112	116
1910–11	120	124	117	123
1911–12	125	125	117	126
1912–13	139	132	124	133
1913–14	146	140	126	133

* F. J. Atkinson's Index Number of Indian prices—111 prices of 48 commodities, weighted (60 articles of food, 19 raw materials, 11 manufactured articles, and 11 imported articles) adjusted to 1898–99 = 100.

† Prices Enquiry Committee—102 articles, weighted, adjusted to 1898–99 = 100.

‡ United Kingdom Labour Department, Board of Trade—47 articles, chiefly raw materials and foodstuffs, weighted—adjusted to 1898–99 = 100.

§ United Kingdom, Sauerbeck—Unweighted Index of 32 commodities, chiefly raw materials and foodstuffs—adjusted to 1898–99 = 100.

CHART I

Indices of Wholesale Prices in India and United Kingdom

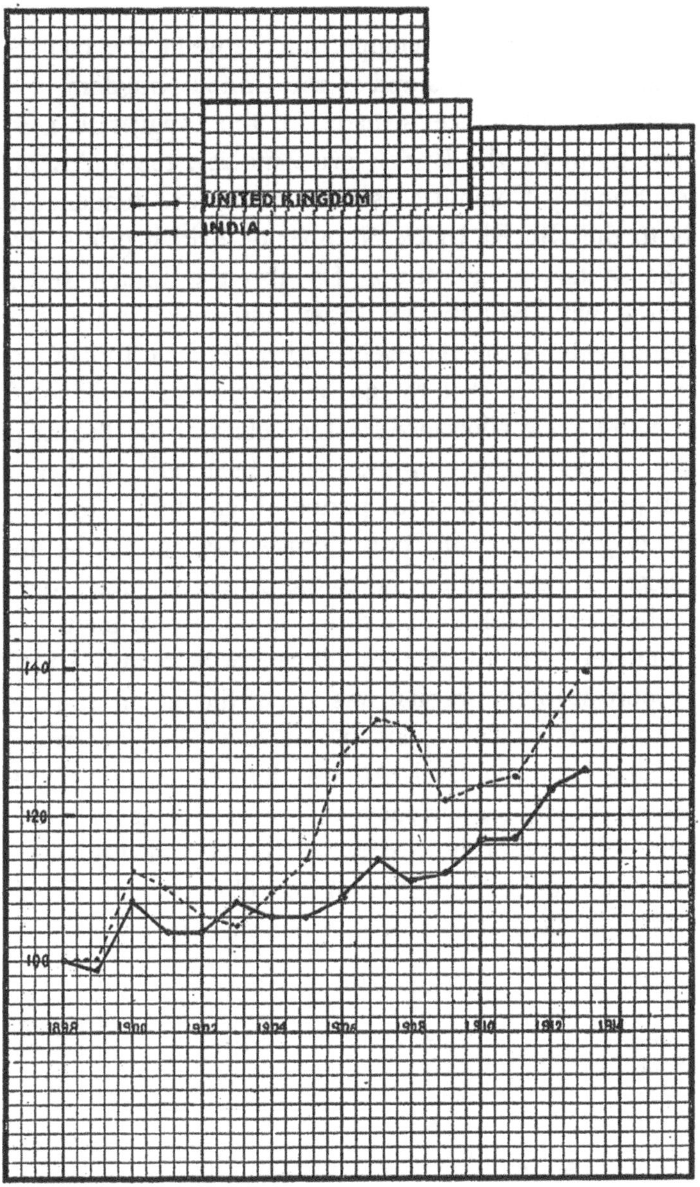

world was more marked in the case of raw materials and food-stuffs than in the case of manufactured articles.[1] The price indices that we shall use are, therefore, likely to exaggerate the rise in British prices.

Chart I represents a comparison between the courses of wholesale prices in India and in the United Kingdom.

Even if no allowance is made for the exaggeration of the upward trend by the British price indices, the Index of the Prices Enquiry Committee shows an upward tendency relatively to the Official Index Number of British prices, except for the solitary year 1903–4. So also the Indian Index as compared with Sauerbeck's Index Number for the United Kingdom reveals the relatively higher level of Indian prices, except in the years 1899 to 1901 and 1902 to 1904. Therefore, if we could make allowance for the defect of the British price indices, Indian prices would have been still higher than British prices throughout the period of our study. How far the relatively greater rise in Indian prices was due to the import of foreign capital, and how far to the increased foreign demand for India's exportable commodities, it is not possible to decide quantitatively. At the same time it cannot be controverted that the import of foreign capital was one of the factors responsible for adding to India's "spendable income" and, consequently, for raising her price-level. Almost the whole of the existing literature on Indian currency and prices seems to have disregarded this factor in attributing the rise of Indian prices solely to the currency policy of the Government. Similarly, writers who have attributed the rise of prices wholly to in-

[1] WORLD RISE IN PRICES

Year	*Foods*	*Raw Materials*	*Manufactured Articles*
1900	100	100	100
1912	134	136	117
1913	126	130	118

R. H. Coats, *Canadian Cost of Living*, Report, vol. ii, p. 247. Quoted by J. Viner, op. cit., p. 221.

creased foreign demand for India's export commodities, are open to the same criticism, though in a lesser degree. Mr. J. M. Keynes only has put forward the theory that "apart from the fluctuations of the seasons, the Indian level of prices is most influenced at the present time (that is 1900–9) by the extent to which Europe makes her investments there."[1] He is understood to have later modified his position to some extent, but still believed that the influence of foreign investments in India on her price-level was appreciable.[2]

SECTIONAL PRICE-LEVELS

The movement of relative price-levels in the borrowing and the lending countries bring about the adjustment of the balances of payment through their effect on the commodity balance of trade. A rising price-level in the borrowing country encourages imports and discourages exports so that the balance of payments due to it is ultimately settled by an excess of commodity imports over exports equal to the volume of its annual foreign borrowings. The method of operation of price changes in the adjustment of the balances of payment can, however, be more clearly understood by comparing the different trends of the sectional price-levels. In passing, however, it need be said that the volume of India's foreign trade is less than 10 per cent of the volume of her domestic trade. Besides, the vast extent of the country, its enormous and immobile population, the sluggish character of its entire economic life make it possible for marked changes to take place in international transactions with much retarded effects on domestic trade. Through long periods foreign exchange, imports and exports, and the prices of imported and exported goods, could vary as if they were quite in a realm of their own, separated by a

[1] J. M. Keynes, "Recent Economic Events in India," *Economic Journal*, 1909, p. 67.

[2] *Report on the Enquiry into the Rise of Prices in India*, vol. i, p. 96.

wide gulf from the prices of Indian domestic goods and from the money incomes of the great mass of people. "Our ascetic ideals and our not very high standard of living prevent the adjustment of our balances by the increase of commodity imports."[1] The sectional price-levels, therefore, cannot be expected to offer any completely reliable proof or disproof of the theory relating to the adjustment of the balances of payment.

Theoretically, the increase in the spendable income of the people in India will cause a rise in the prices of commodities produced for the internal market and of services. The prices of imported commodities will not be appreciably affected by changes in Indian conditions, since they are largely governed by conditions in the producing countries. If anything, the prices of articles imported from the capital-lending country would show a downward tendency. The relative rise in the prices of domestic commodities will not only make imported commodities which are different in kind from the domestic commodities more attractive to the Indian purchaser, but may even lead to a substitution by consumers of imported commodities for domestic commodities of the same class, thus shifting these commodities from the domestic to the import class.[2] Other things being equal, there will also be a decrease in Indian exports. The prices of exportable commodities, except in the few cases where a great proportion of the world's supply is contributed by India, are mainly determined by the "ruling markets" in the consuming countries, ultimately by world-wide relations between supply and demand. The rise in the prices of domestic commodities and services in India will raise the money-cost of production of the export commodities. If the producers succeed in raising the prices of their commodities in sympathy with the increased cost of production, it will lead to a diminution of exports and even to the cessation of exports and the shift of the commodities from the

[1] J. C. Coyajee, *Indian Currency System, 1835–1925*, p. 166.
[2] J. Viner, op. cit., p. 228.

export to the domestic class. If the producers do not succeed in raising the prices of their commodities *pari passu* with the increased cost of production, they would turn to other activities, and in the extreme case the commodities may even shift from the export to the import class. If production in India does not keep pace with the increase in purchasing power a greater proportion of the domestic supply will be consumed in India and thus there will be a reduction in the "surplus" available for export. The ultimate result of all these price changes will be the creation of an unfavourable commodity balance of trade or, what will be more true in the case of India, a reduction in her normal favourable balance by an amount equal to the volume of her annual foreign borrowings.

DOMESTIC, IMPORT, AND EXPORT PRICES IN INDIA

Domestic commodities are commodities which do not enter in significant amounts into international trade either in the form of imports or of exports. The number of such commodities is generally very large, and in all countries probably much exceeds that of commodities having a world range of prices. Many things, such as stone, bricks, timber, etc., because of their great bulk in proportion to their value, are very costly to transport over any considerable distance. Many things, such as milk, butter, eggs, fruits, vegetables, are perishable. "No doubt modern improvements in the transportation of bulky goods and in the preservation of those that are perishable tend to enlarge the sphere of foreign trade. But such things are still sold mainly in their own region and at the prices of their own region."[1] There are also commodities like land and buildings which are immovable, and there are services having limited mobility, because they cannot be separated from the persons rendering them, the prices of which cannot therefore be directly subject to foreign competition. The prices of all

[1] F. W. Taussig, *Free Trade, Tariff, and Reciprocity*, pp. 73, 74.

these commodities as well as services are determined by domestic conditions. In India, which is a continent by itself, the number of commodities belonging to the domestic class

DATA OF CHART II

INDICES OF DOMESTIC, IMPORT, AND EXPORT PRICES

Year	*Domestic Prices—Price of Labour**	*Import Prices—10 Articles Weighted†*	*Export Prices—16 Articles Weighted‡*
1898–99	100	100	100
1899–00	104	98	110
1900–01	108	113	116
1901–02	110	111	114
1902–03	113	109	111
1903–04	115	112	112
1904–05	118	120	119
1905–06	123	120	118
1906–07	127	123	150
1907–08	134	132	139
1908–09	139	126	136
1909–10	145	121	141
1910–11	147	130	158
1911–12	155	139	171
1912–13	157	144	181
1913–14	161	145	193

* Prices Committee Report—Index Number of Wages.

† Compiled from the prices quoted by the Prices Committee Report and by the Department of Statistics in India—10 articles (refined sugar, kerosene, piece-goods—grey, white and coloured; twist and yarn, woollen piece-goods, raw silk, silk piece-goods, liquors) weighted 1898–99 = 100.

‡ Compiled from the prices quoted by the Prices Committee Report and by the Department of Statistics in India—16 articles (rice, wheat, tea, coffee, linseed, til seed, raw cotton, twist and yarn, raw jute and gunny bags, raw wool, dressed skins, raw hides, opium, indigo, rape seed) weighted 1898–99 = 100.

is indefinitely large. The Prices Enquiry Committee have collected price quotations for some of these commodities, but they have not prepared any special index to show the trend of their prices. To prepare a weighted index of domestic commodity prices in India is a very arduous task, and even

CHART II

INDICES OF DOMESTIC, IMPORT, AND EXPORT PRICES

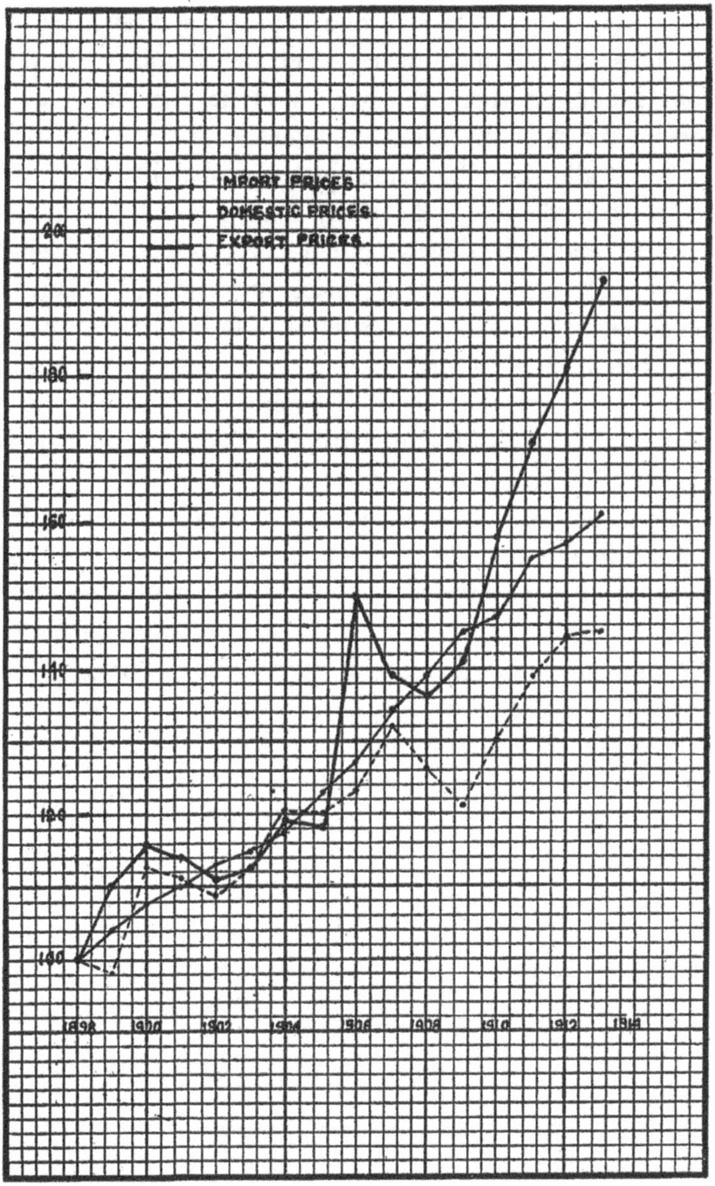

then it will probably not yield satisfactory results because of the incompleteness of the data. However, since the essential requisite of the commodities belonging to the domestic class is their immobility between one country and another, the prices of services which have no greater mobility than the persons rendering them can very well be considered as an important index of the trend of domestic prices. "The trend of wages, if allowance be made for the probability that wages will show considerable inflexibility during periods of fluctuation in general price-levels, offers perhaps the best single index of the trend of domestic prices in general."[1] Therefore in the absence of a special index we shall use the index number of wages in India prepared by the Prices Enquiry Committee to represent the trend of domestic prices. It includes industrial wages and the wages of skilled labourers, unskilled labourers, and domestic servants in urban areas and cities.

To examine the course of import and export prices we have prepared weighted index numbers from the declared wholesale prices of important commodities. The weights assigned are based on the importance of the commodities—according to value—in the import and export trade of India every year during the period of our study.

The course of domestic, import, and export prices in India during 1898 to 1913 is represented in Chart II.

Chart II indicates a general upward trend of all the sectional price-levels. This was due, as already explained, to the world-wide business prosperity that characterized the pre-war period of the present century. But among the prices represented in the Chart, export prices show the greatest rise and import prices the least. The course of domestic prices is midway between the two. The prices of imported articles are determined mainly by the conditions ruling in the country or countries which produce them. As more than 75 per cent of our imports during the period under consideration were

[1] J. Viner, op. cit., p. 247.

from Great Britain, a capital lending country, and as India was a capital borrowing country, theory would expect the prices of domestic commodities in India to rise relatively to the prices of imported commodities. But the rise of export prices over domestic prices is anomalous. The import of capital into India is inconsistent with the tremendous rise in the prices of Indian exports. This suggests, however, that there was some other factor in operation whose influence outweighed the effect of foreign borrowings on Indian prices. In fact, the relatively greater rise in the price of Indian exports was due to the "immensely enhanced" demand for them during the period under study.[1] The demand for our exports was all the while moving up by leaps and bounds; and that is why the volume of our exports increased *pari passu* with the increase in their prices. This fact also explains why the expectation of theory in regard to the effects of foreign borrowings on the sectional price-levels in the borrowing country was not fulfilled by the course of sectional prices in India during 1898 to 1913.

THE GENERALLY PREVAILING EXPLANATION OF THE RISE OF PRICES IN INDIA

Our discussion, though directly concerned with the effect of foreign borrowings, incidentally sheds considerable light upon a very controversial aspect of Indian currency history during the period of our study.

Almost all writers on Indian currency have attempted to analyse and discover the causes of the rise of prices in India during 1898 to 1913. It appears, however, that the primary objective of quite a large section of these writers was to discredit the gold-exchange standard system which was brought into operation in India in 1900. The rise of prices in India was put forward as a definite proof of their contention that

[1] J. C. Coyajee, *The Indian Currency System, 1835–1925*, p. 169.

the gold-exchange standard system was less automatic in its functioning than the gold-standard system, that it left to the Government, which managed the currency organization, a large scope for currency manipulation, and that while it provided plenty of openings for the volume of currency in circulation in the country to expand, there were no methods by which the currency circulation could be contracted automatically. In short, it was maintained that the inflation of currency, the immediate cause of the rise of prices was made possible by the new monetary system, and that it would have been impossible had there been a gold standard and a gold currency instead of a gold-exchange standard with token rupees in circulation.[1] As Professor Nicholson, the foremost critic of the gold-exchange standard system in India, puts it: "In the case of gold, there are natural economic forces which in time must limit the monetary supply and so far the level of prices." Thus the problem of Indian prices during the pure gold-exchange standard period has been assumed by these writers to be essentially connected with the particular type of monetary organization adopted by the country. Foreign borrowings and the increased volume of our exports during the period of our study have not been given any consideration whatsoever as factors affecting currency circulation in India and consequently the prices.[2]

[1] C. N. Vakil and Muranjan, *Currency and Prices in India*, p. 326. "As pointed out already the medium of circulation had now come to depend upon the will of the administrators of the country. It is the acts or the policy of those who govern this country that has determined the course of prices in India ever since 1893."

[2] In their hurry to criticize the Government for what they believe to be the mismanagement of currency without taking into consideration all the relevant factors, writers in India have a good parallel in Argentina. The following passage from a study of *Argentine International Trade Under Inconvertible Paper Money, 1880–1900*, by J. H. Williams, bears out this statement:

"It has been a fairly common remark among Argentine writers on economic problems that the vicissitudes of Argentine paper money history have had nothing to do with borrowing operations, or with

To substantiate their contention that the rise of prices in India was due to the gold-exchange standard and its manipulation by the Government, writers on Indian currency compare the movement of price-levels in India with those of price-levels in Great Britain.[1] But the fact that Indian prices rose relatively to British prices during the period, while it suggests that the divergence may be due to differences in the currency systems does not at all prove it. Had it not been for their preoccupation with the alleged defects of the Indian currency organization, these writers would have looked for less plausible but more reasonable explanations of the divergence. During the period of our study, i.e. 1898 to 1913, India was a capital-importing country, while Great Britain was a capital-exporting country. This difference in the international position of the two countries was itself sufficient to bring about a divergence between the movements of their price-levels.[2] Therefore, this divergence between the prices

the balance of international payments. When in 1890 the gold premium was shooting up by leaps and bounds, the Paris correspondent of *La Nacion* reported to his paper an interview with various European bankers in which the bankers took the view that the crisis, and the premium on gold, was fundamentally due to the inability of Argentina to meet its enormous liabilities of interest owed abroad; the correspondent added the characteristic sentence: 'In Argentina, on the contrary, every one knows that the crisis is due to bad government, to bad political and financial administration, and to excessive issues of paper money.' "

[1] B. R. Ambedkar, *The Problem of the Rupee*, pp. 199–200.

[2] J. Viner, *Canada's Balance of International Indebtedness, 1900–13*, p. 218.

"The countries grouped in ascending order according to the degree of buoyancy which their prices showed are as follows: (i) Great Britain, France, Italy, Belgium, Holland, and Norway; (ii) Germany, Austria, Russia; (iii) India, Australia, New Zealand; (iv) Japan, Hungary, the United States, and Canada. Although it is not to be contended that the international movement of capital is the sole factor determining the trend of price-levels in different countries, it is significant that in general the capital-lending countries experienced the least rise in prices and the capital-borrowing countries the greatest rise."

ruling in India and Great Britain cannot be attributed to the different currency systems of these countries. It was essentially due to their relations in the international capital market and hence cannot be invoked to prove the merits or demerits of a particular system of currency. The trend of prices in Canada and the United States of America lends support to this contention. For both of these countries were on a gold-standard basis and yet the divergence between their price-levels and the price-level in Great Britain during 1898 to 1913 was the greatest. Here, again, the explanation is to be found in the different relations of these countries in the international capital market—Canada and the United States of America were borrowing heavily from Great Britain. Whatever the system of currency obtaining in a country an import of foreign capital is bound to raise its price-level.

Another explanation of the rise of prices in India during the pre-war period, without reference to the particular currency system which existed in the country, is put forward by Sir J. C. Coyajee. He maintains: "Whatever might be the currency system of a country, large gains from international trade make a country of higher level of incomes, and under certain circumstances (e.g. inefficiency of labour in certain directions or prevalence of diminishing returns) of high prices. These factors would be sure to affect prices even under a gold-currency system, especially in an undeveloped country like India, producing mainly raw materials of industry which are subject to the law of diminishing returns."[1] As we already know, due to the general business prosperity of the world and the industrial expansion of a great many countries, the demand for India's export commodities—mainly raw materials—was fast increasing. This increased demand for the export commodities raised their prices, and the rising tendency of prices which reflects the increasing intensity of foreign demand was kept till the outbreak of the war. Naturally the gains of India were

[1] J. C. Coyajee, *The Indian Currency System, 1835–1925*, p. 160.

very large. First, the volume of her exports was increasing and, secondly, her export commodities were being sold at an increasing level of prices. The large favourable balances of trade which were the direct result of this advantageous position of India in the international market were liquidated by the sale of Council Bills. On presentation to the Treasury these bills were cashed in rupees which constituted additions to the volume of currency circulation in the country.[1] Since additions to the currency circulation in India during the period of the gold-exchange standard were made chiefly by means of Council Bills, writers on Indian currency who maintain that there was inflation of currency attributed the phenomenon to the unusually large sale of Council Bills by the Secretary of State. But the sale of Council Bills was only the mechanism by which the impact of outside international forces was being transmitted to the various parts of the internal economy in India, chiefly to the price organization. The demand for Council Bills was really a demand for purchasing power in India, which was created not by the management of her particular currency system, but by her foreign borrowings, and still more, by the increasing international demand for her exports. So long as these factors were active, their influence would have been felt upon the Indian price-level, irrespective of the monetary organization obtaining in the country. And if this is a rational and sufficient explanation of the phenomenon under discussion, surely to establish the statistical fact that Indian prices rose more than the British during the pre-war years of this century, does not at all prove the point that the greater rise of the Indian prices was in any way due to the peculiarity of the Indian currency organization.

It is evident, then, that the true causal sequence ran during the period from the growing and intense demand for a number of Indian products supplemented by foreign borrowings,

[1] For an explanation of the net addition to the currency circulation effected by means of Council Bills, see footnote on p. 153.

through an increase of currency, to the general rise of prices in India. The rise of prices in India was due to her foreign borrowings and to the foreign demand for her export commodities; and it was able to sustain itself over a long period, because the foreign demand for India's export products was becoming more and more intense. The main factor in the situation—the advantageous position which India occupied in her foreign trade—was steadily becoming more conspicuous, through more than a decade of the world's commercial and industrial prosperity.

SUMMARY

The results of the analysis of relative price-levels undertaken in this chapter may be presented as follows:

(i) First, as a result of the increased purchasing power in India due to her foreign borrowings and her advantageous position in foreign trade, there was a rise in the general price-level. At the same time as a result of the diminished purchasing power in Great Britain—the capital-lending country during the period of our study—the rise in her general price-level was relatively less.

(ii) Secondly, the sectional price-levels in India during this period also showed a general upward tendency. Export prices mounted very high, followed by domestic prices and import prices in the order of their buoyancy.

(iii) Finally, export prices displayed the greatest rise because of the increasing foreign demand for India's export commodities during the period, which more than outweighed the influence of foreign borrowings in the opposite direction.

CHAPTER VIII

ADJUSTMENT OF THE BALANCE OF PAYMENT AND THE BARTER TERMS OF TRADE

COMMODITY BALANCE OF TRADE

In bringing about the final adjustment of international balances of indebtedness to more or less permanent disturbances the commodity balance of trade is by far the most important single factor. Specie imports and exports, as items in the commodity balance of trade, are only a preliminary phase in the adjustment. "They exert their main influence, not through the effect on the balance of payments of their own values as debits and credits, but by their influence on price-levels and through them on the remaining items in the commodity balance of trade."[1]

So far as invisible items in the balance of payment are concerned changes in price-levels have no appreciable influence on them. International transactions in services are very little affected by them. Tourists' expenditure and insurance transactions also do not show any influence of the changes in exchange rates and prices. The amount of freight charges payable abroad or receivable from abroad by a given country is directly determined by the volume of its foreign trade, by the proportion in which that trade is carried on by foreign or national shipping companies and by the amount of transportation business done for other countries as well as by freight rates. When factors like continued foreign borrowing from abroad, or increased foreign demand for its export commodities disturb a country's international balance of indebtedness, they affect its balance of freight payments mainly through

[1] J. Viner, op. cit., p. 256.

their influence on the volume of commodity transactions, although they may influence the extent to which that country's capital and labour is engaged in the carrying business. Interest payments are determined simply by the amount of capital borrowings, the rates of interest agreed upon and the extent to which debtors respect their contractual obligations.

Non-commercial transactions like immigrants' and emigrants' remittances and the movements into and out of a country of migrants' personal effects, because of their non-commercial character are wholly free from the influence, direct or indirect, of any factors disturbing the international balance of payments. Only the capital brought in by immigrants is a possible exception. For an increase in foreign borrowings or in the foreign demand for export commodities brings about in the borrowing country a situation favourable to an inflow of foreign labour.[1]

It follows from this that when a disturbing factor of sufficient importance and long-continued duration, such as Indian borrowings abroad during 1898 to 1913, upsets the even balance between her debit and credit international obligations, an even balance of payments is restored and maintained in spite of the debit balance of indebtedness mainly through compensatory variations in the commodity balance of trade. Specie movements and transfers of securities and bank deposits are important in the final adjustment of the balance only when the disturbances to the even balance of payments are casual and temporary. Transfers of securities and bank desposits do not play an important part in the adjustment of the balance of payments to a continued debit or credit balance of indebtedness, since they themselves are merely representative of some

[1] A. C. Whitaker, "The Ricardian Theory of Gold Movements," 18. *Quarterly Journal of Economics, 1904*, p. 231.

"The investment of capital abroad, the travel of tourists, and all the other factors outside of the balance of trade itself are the comparatively independent variables, the balance of trade in goods is the compensatory variable in the balance sheet of total indebtedness."

of the items in the balance of indebtedness to which adjustment must be made.

The shift in the commodity balance of trade necessary to bring about the adjustment of the balance of indebtedness to foreign borrowings is caused, as explained in the preceding chapter, by the influence of changed money incomes and prices on commodity imports and exports. In the borrowing country the money incomes and prices rise, while in the lending country they fall. In the borrowing country the prices of imported articles tend to go down, while the prices of domestic and exported articles tend to rise. The falling prices of the imported articles and the rising money incomes encourage imports, while the rising prices of the exported commodities discourage exports. This process, provided the annual amount of foreign borrowings remains constant, brings about an unfavourable commodity balance of trade or a reduction in the normal favourable balance of trade equal to that amount. Thus ultimately foreign capital enters the borrowing country in the form of commodities. We have already seen that changes in the sectional price-levels of India as a result of her foreign borrowings would have been as predicted by theory but for the simultaneous influence of another factor, viz. increased foreign demand for India's export commodities. Now, let us see how far the commodity imports and exports of India were affected by changes in her sectional price-levels, and how far the adjustment of the balance of indebtedness to foreign borrowings was brought about according to the expectations of theory. The relevant data are presented in Table XXXII.

In trying to find out a correlation between India's foreign borrowings and her commodity imports and exports as given in the following table a crucial point must not be lost sight of. When the theory states that the ultimate adjustment of the balance of indebtedness to foreign borrowings is brought about by a shift in the commodity balance of trade it assumes certain things. First, it assumes that before a country begins to raise foreign loans there exists an even balance between her credit and debit obligations and, secondly, that the foreign borrowings continue for a long period at an even rate. In the case of India during the period of our study the second of these assumptions did not hold good. Both the direct as well as the

TABLE XXXII

COMMODITY IMPORTS AND EXPORTS, FOREIGN BORROWINGS AND THE SALE OF COUNCIL BILLS

(*In lakhs of rupees*)

Year	*Commodity Imports*	*Commodity Exports*	*Foreign Borrowings*	*Council Bills Sold by the Secretary of State*
1898–99	8,465	12,021	409	2,808
1899–00	9,004	11,704	1,225	2,848
1900–01	9,902	12,193	1,308	1,998
1901–02	10,150	13,636	1,337	2,783
1902–03	10,318	13,893	577	2,775
1903–04	12,311	16,845	179	3,568
1904–05	13,571	17,425	1,190	3,654
1905–06	14,447	17,730	2,497	4,722
1906–07	15,512	18,274	1,029	4,989
1907–08	17,088	18,264	2,668	2,292
1908–09	14,213	15,945	1,428	2,096
1909–10	15,217	19,437	2,465	4,102
1910–11	16,567	21,708	728	3,955
1911–12	18,768	23,835	565	4,037
1912–13	21,541	25,685	535	3,850
1913–14	22,013	25,609	1,831	4,660

indirect estimates of India's foreign borrowings clearly show that their annual flow was subject to large variations.

Bearing in mind this divergence between the conditions assumed by theory and those existing in India, if we scan the course of India's commodity imports, we find that they were increasing every year during 1898–99 to 1913–14 except in 1908–9. It is not possible to find out how much of the increase in imports was due to foreign borrowings and to the unusual prosperity of our exporters, separately, but it can be safely assumed that it was in part at least the result of India's capital imports during the period. This much for the part played by the relatively low prices of imported articles and the increasing spendable income of the people in India. However, the adjustment of the balance of indebtedness to foreign borrowings according to theory is brought about not only by an increase in imports but also by a decrease in exports. Naturally, therefore, simultaneously with the increase in India's imports, we should expect a decrease in her exports, if the mechanism of adjustment in India is to serve as a verification of deductive theory. But the figures of commodity exports from India reveal an entirely different state of affairs. Simultaneously with the increase in commodity imports, there was a much larger increase in commodity exports and this in spite of the fact that the export prices in India during 1898 to 1913 displayed the greatest rise. If foreign borrowings were the only factor disturbing the even balance between India's credit and debit obligations then we should have expected a reduction in the total value of Indian exports. That this did not happen, but that there was on the contrary an increase in Indian exports, suggests that some other powerful factor was in operation, tending all the time to over-balance the effect of foreign borrowings. This factor, as we have seen in the previous chapter, was an increasing demand for Indian exports. Had it not been for the intervention of this factor, the rising prices of export commodities due to the increased spendable income in India consequent upon her foreign borrowings might be expected to have reduced her commodity exports. As it was, the adjustment of India's balance of payments to the inflow of foreign funds was effected largely, possibly wholly, by an increase in her imports.

We, therefore, conclude that the process of adjustment of India's balance of indebtedness to her foreign borrowings was to a great extent obscured by the increasing demand for her export commodities which set in at the beginning of the present century and continued till the outbreak of the war. In the absence of this factor, the adjustment of India's balance of trade to her varying foreign borrowings would have been brought about under the Gold Exchange Standard, subject to the peculiar conditions of Indian economic life, in exactly the same manner as it is effected under the pure Gold Standard.

FOREIGN BORROWINGS AND THE TERMS OF INTERNATIONAL EXCHANGE

According to Mill, during a period of foreign borrowings prices rise in the borrowing country and fall in the lending country. It is a corollary of this reasoning that during a period of foreign borrowings the terms of international exchange, or to use Professor Taussig's expression, "the barter terms of trade,"[1] should move in favour of the borrowing country and against the lending country—in other words, that the borrowing country obtains more of imported goods in exchange for each unit of its exports than it did before the foreign borrowings set in. This shift in the barter terms of trade which represents a shift in the reciprocal demand of borrowing and lending countries for each other's products is essential to the adjustment of the balance of indebtedness to foreign borrowings, both under barter and money exchange. However, under barter, the transfer of loans to the borrowing country in the form of goods comes first and is the cause and not the effect of the shift in the terms of international exchange. The shift in the terms of international exchange serves to restore equilibrium in the trade in those commodities which are not directly connected with foreign borrowings. Under money exchange the shift in the barter terms of trade is the condition precedent

[1] Professor A. C. Pigou expresses this quantitative relation between commodity imports and exports by the phrase "real rates of international interchange."

to the coming in of foreign borrowings in the form of goods.

An increased foreign demand for the export commodities of a country has a similar influence on its barter terms of trade as foreign borrowings. In the case of India, therefore, where both the factors were operating simultaneously during the period of our study, we should expect the barter terms of trade to move to her advantage.

THE BARTER TERMS OF TRADE

There are two ways of looking at the barter terms of trade. One may be indicated by the phrase "net barter terms of trade"; the other by the "gross barter terms of trade." The first takes into consideration those goods only which pay for goods, while the second regards the whole volume of goods, both imports and exports.[1] The net barter terms are those of the exchange of domestic goods for foreign goods in the simplest case, where the international trade is concerned only with the purchase and sale of merchandise. In modern times the international trade of a country includes, besides merchandise transactions, a large volume of non-merchandise transactions. Therefore, the net barter terms of trade have now become a purely theoretical concept. The actual international trade of any modern country can be separated into two parts: first, the exchange of exported goods for an equal money value of imported goods; second, an excess in money value of imported goods over the exported goods or vice versa, representing the balance of non-merchandise transactions. This distinction is theoretical only. What actually happens is that one "unsegregated mass" of physical goods flows into the country as imports and another mass flows out as exports. A country having a credit balance of payments on "invisible" account receives a larger money value of imports than that of

[1] F. W. Taussig, *International Trade*, p. 113.

its exports, and a country in the reverse position pays out a larger money value of exports than that of her imports. The physical volume of the imported goods as compared with the physical volume of the exported goods will be greater for the country having an excess of imports in money value and smaller for the country having an excess of exports. This relation between the whole of a country's physical imports and exports which we encounter in fact constitutes the "gross barter terms of trade."

THE MEASUREMENT OF THE BARTER TERMS OF TRADE

The barter terms of trade must always be advantageous to all the countries having trade relations because the terms must lie within the limits fixed by the comparative costs of production. Otherwise the countries which do not get any advantage from an international exchange of goods would not enter into international trade at all. However, the advantages of an international exchange may not be equally shared by the countries concerned at any time and may be shared by any one country differently at different times. Therefore, a shift in the "barter terms of trade" of a country to its advantage or disadvantage means more favourable terms or less favourable terms than before. The terms on which a country barters its imports for its exports cannot be measured, but the modifications which may arise in these terms and which the theorists have in mind when they say that the terms of trade generally move in favour of the borrowing country and against the lending country, can be measured. As Professor Taussig says: "They only indicate in which direction the accretion of gain—from international exchange—is changing; whether the gain, whatever it be in a given year, is less or greater in that year than in previous years or in subsequent years. It is changes and changes alone, both in the net barter terms of trade and in the gross barter terms, which we are able to follow." The barter terms of trade can be said to have moved in favour of India if the quantity of exported goods paid in exchange for a given quantity of imported goods shows a decrease during the period of our study, as compared with the quantity of exported goods paid in 1898. To put it in another way, the barter terms of trade can be said to have moved in favour of India if the quantity of imported goods received in exchange for a given quantity of exported goods shows an increase during the period as compared with the quantity of imported goods received in 1898. On the other hand, the barter terms of trade can be said to have moved against India if the quantity of exported goods paid in exchange for a given quantity of imported goods shows an increase or if the quantity of imported goods received in exchange for a given quantity of exported goods shows a decrease during the period, as compared with the respective ratios prevailing in 1898.

INDIA'S NET BARTER TERMS OF TRADE

The net barter terms of trade take into account only those goods which pay for goods. Therefore, as the foreign trade of a country is carried on in terms of money values, the value of goods imported and the value of goods exported in exchange must always be equal. Thus if the imports and exports in each single year are the same in money value, it follows that a change in import and export prices indicates accurately a change in physical quantity.[1] If export prices fall relatively to import prices it means that more of exports are exchanged for a given quantity of imports and vice versa. The relative changes in India's net barter terms of trade can, therefore, be ascertained by forming an index number of the ratio between her import and export prices with the ratio of 1898

[1] A. L. Bowley, *England's Foreign Trade in the Nineteenth Century*, p. 20.

as the basis.[1] However, it need hardly be said that the supposition underlying this aspect of the barter terms of trade does not conform to reality. The imports and exports of India were never equal in money value and, hence, her net barter terms of trade are merely a hypothetical matter.

INDIA'S GROSS BARTER TERMS OF TRADE

The gross barter terms of trade which take into account the whole of a country's imports as compared with the whole of its exports, represent the real terms on which that country exchanges her export commodities. Therefore, the direction of changes in those terms will be an accurate index as to whether the advantage of international exchange was shifting in her favour or against her during 1898 to 1913. To ascertain the relative changes in India's gross barter terms of trade we adjust the values of imports and exports every year during the period of our study to their respective prices prevailing in the year 1898. The new values would then represent the values of the physical volume of goods imported and exported as they would have been if prices had remained unchanged since 1898. Thus prices being reduced to a common basis a larger or smaller money value would necessarily represent a

[1] The method can be more easily explained by means of an equation:

The value of goods imported X = the quantity of goods imported Y, $\times$ the import prices, m.

The value of goods exported X^1 = the quantity of goods exported Y^1, $\times$ the export prices, m^1.

The net barter terms of trade = the quantity of goods exported $\div$ the quantity of goods imported $= \frac{Y^1}{Y}$.

But since
$$X^1 = X$$
$$Y^1 m^1 = Ym.$$
$$\therefore \frac{Y^1}{Y} = \frac{m}{m^1} = \text{import prices} \div \text{export prices.}$$

larger or smaller volume of physical goods.[1] The adjusted figures of money values become measures of physical quantities. If, therefore, we take the proportion of imports to exports in 1898 as 100 and deduce the change in that ratio for the other years, we shall get an accurate index of changes in India's gross barter terms of trade. We say it once more that here as well as in the figures regarding the net barter terms of trade there is nothing which tells us whether the terms are in themselves favourable for any given year. They indicate only the direction and extent of changes.

The Index Numbers of India's "net barter terms of trade" and "gross barter terms of trade," prepared according to the methods explained above, are presented in Table XXXIII.

The net barter terms of trade as well as the gross barter terms of trade as indicated by their respective index numbers were moving to the greater and greater advantage of India throughout the period of our study, except during one or two years, when they seem to have moved against India. A given physical quantity of imports was being purchased for a steadily declining physical quantity of exports. But, though the general trend of the barter terms of trade is favourable to India, there were variations in them in particular years. Both these phenomena, the movement of the barter terms of trade against India in certain years and their irregular, though, on the whole, favourable tendency during the period, are due to the intermittent character of the operating influences, viz. the foreign borrowings and the foreign demand for export commodities. However, as the general trend of the barter terms of trade was favourable to India, the expectations of theory in regard to the effect of foreign borrowings and increased foreign demand for export commodities are fully realized.

During the pre-war period of the present century not only

[1] The value of a commodity is determined by its quantity and price. If the price remains constant any change in the value of that commodity must be due wholly to a change in the quantity.

TABLE XXXIII

India's Barter Terms of Trade, 1898–1903

Year	Commodity Imports				Commodity Exports				Index Number of the Net Barter Terms of Trade	Index Number of the Gross Barter Terms of Trade VIII ÷ IV
			Established Values at 1898 Prices				Established Values at 1898 Prices			
	Declared Value	Import Price Index	Absolute Value	Relative Value	Declared Value	Export Price Index	Absolute Value	Relative Value		
	I Rs. 1,00,000	II 1898=100	III Rs. 1,00,000	IV 1898=100	V Rs. 1,00,000	VI 1898=100	VII Rs. 1,00,000	VIII 1898=100	IX 1898=100	X 1898=100
1898–99	8,465	100	8,465	100	12,021	100	12,021	100	100	100
1899–00	9,004	98	9,188	109	11,704	110	10,640	89	89	82
1900–01	9,902	113	8,763	104	12,193	116	10,511	87	97	84
1901–02	10,150	111	9,114	108	13,636	114	11,961	100	97	94
1902–03	10,318	109	9,466	112	13,893	111	12,516	104	98	93
1903–04	12,311	112	10,991	130	16,845	112	15,040	125	100	96
1904–05	13,571	120	11,309	134	17,425	119	14,643	122	101	91
1905–06	14,447	120	12,039	142	17,730	118	15,025	125	102	88
1906–07	15,512	123	12,611	149	18,274	150	12,183	101	82	68
1907–08	17,088	132	12,945	153	18,264	139	13,139	109	96	71
1908–09	14,213	126	11,280	133	15,945	136	11,724	98	93	74
1909–10	15,217	121	12,576	149	19,437	141	13,721	114	86	76
1910–11	16,567	130	12,743	151	21,708	158	13,739	114	82	75
1911–12	18,768	139	13,502	160	23,835	171	13,939	116	81	73
1912–13	21,541	144	14,959	177	25,685	181	14,191	118	80	67
1913–14	22,013	145	15,181	179	25,609	193	13,269	110	75	61

India but all countries mainly exporting raw materials were gaining heavily because of the fall of freights and the constantly growing demand for their products from industrial countries where new industries were being rapidly established. During the same period the barter terms of trade moved to the disadvantage of the industrial countries. For Great Britain, the chief industrial country of the pre-war period, the barter terms of trade became more and more advantageous between 1880 and 1900. But after 1900 the terms of trade were moving against her, right till the outbreak of the war.[1] As Dr. Marshall has observed, countries in the position of India "have gained all round: they have gained by lower cost of transport, and they have gained by the lower cost of manufacture of commodities for direct use; and that almost equally whether these goods are manufactured by themselves or imported. For competition compels England, Germany, and other Western countries to give to consumers almost at once the full benefit of any economy in manufacturing which they have obtained." Moreover, the countries whose gains from international exchange displayed an upward tendency were mostly the capital-borrowing countries, while the countries whose gains were diminishing were mostly the capital-lending countries.

MONEY WAGES AND THE BARTER TERMS OF TRADE

The concrete way in which the inhabitants of a country obtain the benefit of more favourable terms of trade—net or gross—is that their money incomes rise while the prices of imported commodities fall, or rise more than the prices of imports. With the same amount of labour they can purchase more of imported goods. Hence we should expect the increasing advantage obtained by India during 1898 to 1913 to be associated with a rise in money wages. The trends of the curves representing

[1] F. W. Taussig, "The Changes in Great Britain's Foreign Trade Terms after 1900." 35. *Economic Journal, 1925.*

DATA OF CHART III

Indices of Money Wages and the Barter Terms of Trade

Year	*Index Number of Money Wages*	*Index Number of the Net Barter Terms of Trade*	*Index Number of the Gross Barter Terms of Trade*
1898–99	100	100	100
1899–00	104	89	82
1900–01	108	97	84
1901–02	110	97	94
1902–03	113	98	93
1903–04	115	100	96
1904–05	118	101	91
1905–06	123	102	88
1906–07	127	82	68
1907–08	134	96	71
1908–09	139	93	74
1909–10	145	86	76
1910–11	147	82	75
1911–12	155	81	73
1912–13	157	80	67
1913–14	161	75	61

the money wages and the barter terms of trade—net as well as gross—drawn in Chart III justify this expectation. It clearly shows the natural inverse[1] correlation between the money wages and the terms of trade.

[1] This is because the terms of trade are calculated as $= \frac{\text{Exports}}{\text{Imports}}$.

CHART III

INDICES OF MONEY WAGES AND THE BARTER TERMS OF TRADE

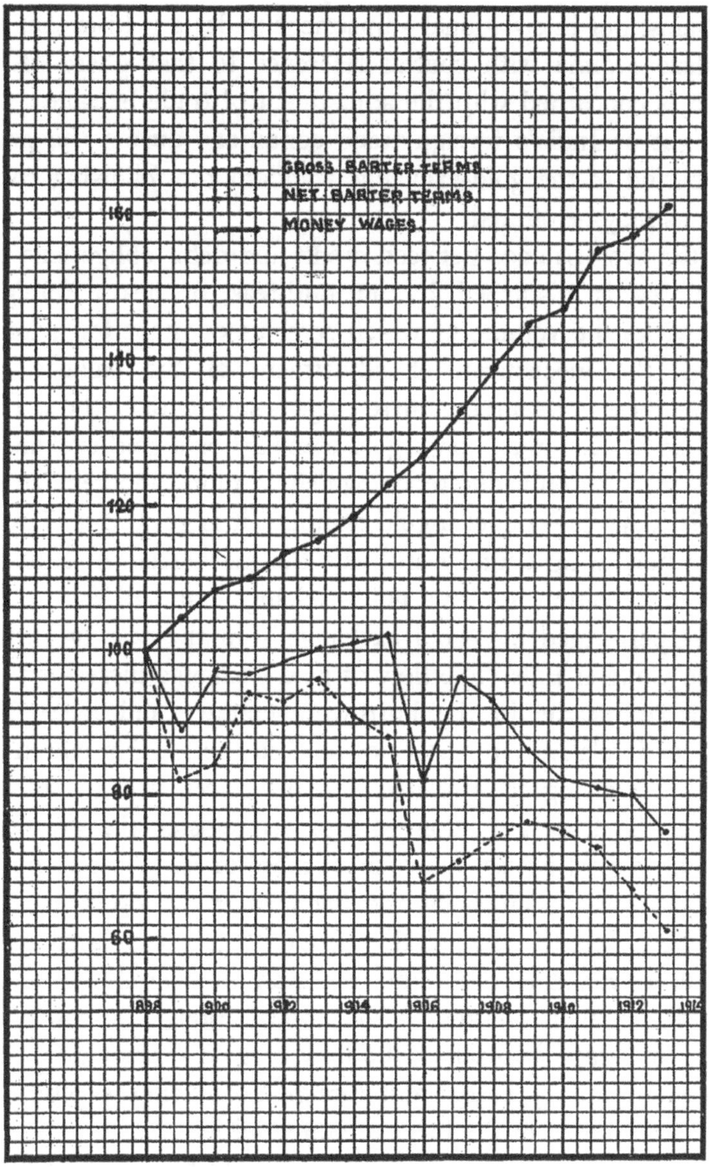

CONCLUSION

The main purpose of this study has been to follow the mechanism of international adjustment under a gold-exchange standard regime with special reference to that phase of it which is concerned with the adjustment of trade balances. In the light of India's foreign trade conditions during the pre-war period of the gold-exchange standard the following conclusions may be offered.

If the even balance between credit and debit obligations of a country is disturbed by an outbreak of heavy foreign borrowings the volume of which remains constant for a long period, the mechanism of adjustment of the balance of indebtedness to its foreign borrowings is substantially the same, whether the country is on a gold standard or a gold-exchange standard. The only difference, which is more apparent than real, is that while under a gold standard it is gold which flows to the borrowing country and sets the mechanism of adjustment in operation, under a gold-exchange standard the function is performed by "gold exchange"—in the case of India by the Council Bills. The flow of gold exchange increases the spendable income in the borrowing country and raises its price-level relatively to the price-level in the lending country. In the borrowing country itself import prices tend to fall or register the least rise, domestic prices register the greatest rise, and export prices follow them more or less closely. As a result of these changes in the sectional price-levels of the borrowing country, commodity imports are stimulated and exports restricted, so that there results an unfavourable balance of trade equal in volume to the annual foreign borrowings. When this stage is reached the flow of gold exchange to the borrowing country ceases and foreign borrowings practically enter the country in the form of commodities.

The working of this mechanism of adjustment of India's

balance of indebtedness to her foreign borrowing during the period of our study was greatly obscured, especially in the latter half of the period by another factor—viz. increased foreign demand for India's export commodities—more powerful than foreign borrowings. Therefore the restrictive effect of higher domestic prices and consequently of higher costs of production on commodity exports, caused by the transfer of a part of foreign borrowings to India in the form of spendable income, was more than counter-balanced by a simultaneous increase in the foreign demand for them. So far as the other steps of the mechanism of adjustment are concerned, both the factors disturbing the even balance between India's credit and debit obligations during the period were working in the same direction. It is not possible to single out either of these factors and trace its effects on Indian prices and money wages and ultimately on the commodity balance of trade. Hence, bearing in mind the various stages in the process of adjustment of balances of indebtedness to foreign borrowings under a gold-standard system, we have tried to find out if the mechanism was different under a gold-exchange standard system, and wherever it was found to be different we have tried to discover if the difference was due to the other factor operating on India's foreign trade during the same period. The theoretical conclusions drawn from this study cannot, therefore, be considered as clearly brought out from the Indian case. They are essentially tentative in character.

Besides, the peculiarities of India's economic life in general serve as a still further qualification to the conclusions offered above. The vast extent of the country, its enormous immobile population, the sluggish character of its entire economic life make it possible for marked changes to take place in international transactions with much retarded effects on domestic trade. Through long periods foreign exchange, imports and exports, and the prices of imported and exported goods can vary as if they were quite in a realm of their own, separated by a wide gulf from the prices of Indian domestic goods and from the money incomes of the great mass of people. Economic adjustments take place slowly in India, but that they are governed by the same laws and occur in the same manner as elsewhere cannot be disproved.

PROFESSOR FINDLAY SHIRRAS'S METHOD OF ASCERTAINING FREIGHT CHARGES

WE shall discuss here some of the methods which have been used by previous writers in calculating the freight charges paid by India on her foreign trade. Professor Shirras calculates the freight charges on India's foreign trade in 1922–23. His calculation is based upon a study of the earnings of British shipping on different trade routes in 1913, made by the Board of Trade.[1] According to the Board of Trade study, 9 per cent of the total British shipping earnings in 1913 were realized on the Indian trade route. Professor Shirras assumes that this percentage was true for the year 1922–23 also, and estimates that on this assumption the earnings of British shipping on the Indian trade route in 1922–23 amounted to Rs. 15 crores approximately.[2] This, according to Professor Shirras, is equivalent to the sum that India paid on account of freight charges on her foreign trade.

Professor Shirras's method is open to one fundamental criticism. It cannot be said with any justification that the percentage of Great Britain's freight earnings on the Indian route to her total earnings on all routes remained constant between 1913–14 and 1922–23, or that it was the same for the years 1913 and 1922, in the face of the facts that:

(i) The percentage of British tonnage engaged in Indian trade in 1922–23 was not the same as in 1913, and that

[1] *Board of Trade Journal*, February 3, 1921.

[2] "India's share of the total earnings of the United Kingdom shipping was 9 per cent [in 1913]. Taking that proportion for the year 1922 . . . this would give us a figure of Rs. 15 crores as the gross earnings of British shipping [from Indian trade] during the year." G. Findlay Shirras, *Proceedings of the Seventh Indian Economic Conference*, p. 77.

(ii) The relation between cargo available and the amount of tonnage engaged changed between the two years.

To Great Britain her mercantile marine is a monopoly concern and hence amenable to the laws of monopoly profits. The amount of shipping tonnage and the level of freight rates on a particular trade route are largely determined by the condition of demand on the other trade routes which is ever changing. Thus, if the amount of shipping tonnage and freight rates on different trade routes are constantly fluctuating it is very likely that the shares of Great Britain's freight earnings on each of these routes might have considerably changed during the period 1913 to 1922. This general observation is still more true in the case of India. The employment of shipping on this route seems to have become much less economical in 1922 than in 1913 and the tonnage had become greater in proportion to the cargo available.[1] Hence, to suppose that 9 per cent of the total freight earnings of Great Britain every year are contributed by the Indian route because such was the case in a particular year appears to be illogical and incorrect.

S. N. HAJI'S METHOD

A similar percentage method has also been used by S. N. Haji, but only to confirm the results he obtained by other methods. Nevertheless as a method, unless justified, it is faulty even for corroboration. S. N. Haji takes us back to the days of Sir Robert Giffen, who in the year 1882 calculated that approximately 10 per cent of the value of a commodity should be assigned to freight and insurance charges. Haji accepts this percentage to be true even for the year 1921–22—forty years after Sir Giffen's calculation—and allowing for insurance and other charges takes 8 per cent of the value of a commodity to represent freight charges. What is still more surprising is that

[1] A. J. Sargent, *Seaways of the Empire*, p. 70.

he even procures a remarkable confirmation of this 8 per cent rate from the *ad valorem* percentage of freight charges to imports for the year 1921–22. It is, however, easy to discover from the data he has presented that his corroborative *ad valorem* percentage is unweighted, which makes all the difference between confirmation and disproof.[1] The objections to using Sir Robert Giffen's freight percentage, which had no relation whatsoever to the conditions of trade, shipping, and freights prevailing in the year 1921–22, seem to be stronger than they were for the percentage used by Findlay Shirras. Since the time of Robert Giffen vast changes had taken place in the position of the shipping industry. Freights have been cut down drastically, the tonnage of steamships had been greatly augmented, and the transition from sailing vessels to steel steamships had been almost completely effected. The efficiency of the steam tonnage has been enormously increased in recent years both in regard to speed and carrying capacity; indeed, practically the whole of the British Mercantile Marine was rebuilt during the first decade of the twentieth century.[2]

One more questionable point in the use of Giffen's percentage by Haji is that he has applied it to India's imports as well as exports. It is a well-known fact that inward freight rates and outward freight rates display large differences. Sometimes these differences are so large that the loss in inward freights is made up by the profits on outward freights and vice versa.[3] If this statement is true, it follows that the *ad valorem* percentage of freight charges to import values might have been different from the *ad valorem* percentage of freight

[1] S. N. Haji, *Economics of Shipping*, p. 324.

[2] *Quarterly Review*, July 1911, p. 53.

[3] *The Economist*, February 18, 1899, "Commercial History and Review of 1898":

"For some years outward and homeward freights have reflected on each other an inverse ratio, that when the rates have been good outwards they have declined homeward and vice versa." Also the same supplement for February 18, 1913.

charges to export values. Moreover, as the commodities imported and commodities exported are different, having different values per unit, the percentage of freight charges to imports and exports, even if the rate per ton be the same, will be different.

APPENDIX II

SAVINGS PER HEAD BROUGHT BY IMMIGRANTS FROM DIFFERENT COLONIES

Year	I *Natal* *Rs.*	II *Fiji* *Rs.*	III *Trinidad* *Rs.*	IV *Mauritius* *Rs.*
1898–99	—	230	—	—
1899–00	—	—	216	—
1900–01	—	—	—	—
1901–02*	285	—	—	—
1902–03	—	270	—	30
1903–04	—	308	—	19
1904–05	—	300	—	26
1905–06	—	—	237	8
1906–07	—	483	—	8
1907–08	—	285	—	3
1908–09	75	—	375	—
1908–10	105	—	375	—
1910–11†	105	—	—	—
1911–12	—	—	—	—
1912–13‡	135	315	—	—
1913–14§	135	360	135	—

* 1901–02 Reunion and Guadeloupe .. .. Rs. 135.
† 1910–11 Surinam .. .. Rs. 840.
‡ 1912–13 Demerara .. .. Rs. 195.
§ 1913–14 Demerara, Jamaica, and Surinam .. Rs. 150.

APPENDIX III

REMITTANCES PER HEAD BY RESIDENT INDIAN EMIGRANTS IN THE VARIOUS COLONIES

Year	*Natal* *Rs.*	*Fiji* *Rs.*
1903–04	20	2
1904–05	17	1
1905–06	16	2
1906–07	15	1
1907–08	15	1
1908–09	8	1
1909–10	9	1
1910–11	10	1
1911–12	9	1
1912–13	10	—
1913–14	10	—

BIBLIOGRAPHY

AMBEDKAR, B. R.: *Problem of the Rupee*. London, 1923.

ANGELL, J. W.: *The Theory of International Prices*. Cambridge, 1926.
Review of Viner's *Canada's Balance of International Indebtedness*, *Political Science Quarterly*. 1925.

ANSTEY, V.: *The Trade of the Indian Ocean*. London, 1929.

ATKINSON, F. J.: "Rupee Prices in India, 1870 to 1908." *Journal of the Royal Statistical Society*. 1909.

BASTABLE, C. F.: *The Theory of International Trade*. London, 4th Edition, 1903.

BENHAM, F. C.: Review of Wood's *Borrowing and Business in Australia*, *Economic Journal*. 1931.

BEVERIDGE, WILLIAM H.: *Tariffs, The Case Examined*. London, 1931.

BOGGS, T. H.: *International Trade Balance in Theory and Practice*. New York, 1922.

BORDES, J. VAN WALRE DE: *The Austrian Crown*. London, 1924.

BOWLEY, A. L.: *England's Trade in the Nineteenth Century*. London, 1904.

BULLOCK, C. J., WILLIAMS, J. H., AND TUCKER, R. S.: "The Balance of Trade of the United States." *Review of Economic Statistics*. July 1919.

BURNETT HURST, A. R.: "Lancashire and the Indian Market." *Journal of the Royal Statistical Society*. 1932.

CAIRNES, J. E.: *Leading Principles of Political Economy*. London, 1874.

CANNAN, EDWIN: *Balance of Trade Delusions*. London, 1931.
The Paper Pound of 1797–1821. London, 1919.
A reprint of the Bullion Report of 1810, with comments.

CASSEL, GUSTAV: *Money and Foreign Exchange after 1914*. London, 1922.
The World's Monetary Problems. London, 1921.

COWDEN, D. J.: *Measures of Exports of the United States*. New York, 1931. *Studies in History, Economics and Public Law*, edited by the Faculty of Political Science, Columbia University.

COYAJEE, J. C.: *The Indian Currency System*. Madras, 1930.

CRAMMOND, EDGAR: "British Investments Abroad." *Quarterly Review*. July 1907 and 1911.

DANIELS, G. W., AND JEWKES, J.: "The Crisis in the Lancashire Cotton Industry." *Economic Journal*. 1927.

EDGEWORTH, F. Y.: *Papers Relating to Political Economy*, vol. ii.

EDWARDS, G. W.: *International Trade Finance*. New York, 1926.

FEIS, H.: *Europe: the World's Banker, 1870–1914*. New Haven, 1930.

FLUX, A. W.: "The British Export Trade." *Economic Journal*. 1927.

"Measurement of Price Changes." *Journal of the Royal Statistical Society*. 1921.

"Comparability of Statistics: Need for Uniformity." *The Times Trade and Engineering Supplement*. May 21, 1932.

GIFFEN, SIR ROBERT: *Economic Inquiries and Studies*. 2 Volumes. London, 1904.

GRAHAM, F. D.: *Currency, Prices and Exchange in Hyper-Inflated Germany, 1924–26*.

"International Trade under Depreciated Paper: The United States, 1862–79." *Quarterly Journal of Economics*. 1922.

"The Theory of International Values Re-examined." *Quarterly Journal of Economics*. 1923.

HAJI, S. N.: *Economics of Shipping*. Bombay, 1924.

HARROD, R. F.: *International Economics*. London, 1933.

HAWTREY, R. G.: *Currency and Credit*. 1928.

HOBSON, C. K.: "British Investments Overseas." *Annals of the American Academy of Social Science*. November 1926.

"Measurements of the Balance of Trade." *Economica*. May 1921.

The Export of Capital. London, 1914.

HOBSON, J. A.: *Economic Interpretation of Investment*. London, 1911.

International Trade. London, 1904.

HOLLANDER, J. H.: "International Trade under Depreciated Paper." *Quarterly Journal of Economics*. 1918.

HOWARD, H. F.: *India and the Gold Standard*. Calcutta, 1911.

HUME, DAVID: *Essays, Moral, Political and Literary*.

JEVONS, H. S.: *Future of Exchange and Indian Currency*. London, 1922.

JOSHI, R. M.: *Indian Export Trade*. 1922.

KEMMERER, E. W.: *Modern Currency Reforms*. 1916.

KEYNES, J. M.: "Recent Economic Events in India." *Economic Journal*. 1909.
"Alfred Marshall, 1842–1924." *Economic Journal*. 1924.
Indian Currency and Finance. London, 1924.

LAUGHLIN, J. L.: "Prices and the International Movement of Specie." *Journal of Political Economy*. 1902.

LAVINGTON, F.: *The English Capital Market*.

LAYTON, W. T.: *An Introduction to the Study of Prices*. London, 1922.

LEHFELDT, R. A.: "The Rate of Interest on British and Foreign Investments." *Journal of the Royal Statistical Society*. 1913. *Journal of the Royal Statistical Society*. 1914.

LEXIS, W.: "The Agio on Gold and International Trade." *Economic Journal*. 1895.

LORIA, A.: "Notes on the Theory of International Trade. *Economic Journal*. 1901.

LOVEDAY, A.: *The History and Economics of Indian Famines*. London, 1914.

MARSHALL, ALFRED: *Money, Credit and Commerce*. London, 1923.
"The Pure Theory of Foreign Trade." No. 1 series of scarce tracts in Economic and Political Science.

MILL, J. S.: *Principles of Political Economy*. London, 1848.

MITCHELL, W. C.: *Business Cycles*. 1930.

MORELAND, W. H.: "The Indian Prices Enquiry." *Economic Journal*. 1916.

MORRISON, SIR THEODORE: *Economic Transition in India*. London, 1916.

MULHALL, M. G.: *The Dictionary of Statistics*. Fourth Edition, London, 1903.

MUN, THOMAS: *England's Treasure by Foreign Trade*. London, 1664. A Reprint.

NICHOLSON, J. S.: "The Report on Indian Currency in Relation to the Gold Exchange Standard. *Economic Journal.* 1914.

PAISH, SIR GEORGE: "Great Britain's Investments in Other Lands." *Journal of the Royal Statistical Society.* 1909. *Journal of the Royal Statistical Society.* 1911.

PIGOU, A. C.: *Essays in Applied Economics.*

PIGOU AND ROBERTSON: *Economic Essays and Addresses.* London, 1931.

PILLAI, P.: *Economic Conditions in India.* London, 1925.

RAU, B. R.: *Present-Day Banking in India.* Third Edition. Calcutta, 1930.

"Can India Become a Creditor Country?" *Proceedings of the Fifteenth Indian Economic Conference.* 1932.

RICARDO, DAVID: *The Principles of Political Economy and Taxation.* Everyman's Library Edition.

SANYAL: *Development of Indian Railways.*

SARGENT, A. J.: *Seaways of the Empire.* London, 1930.

SCHLULER, W. C.: *The Pre-War Business Cycles, 1907–14.* New York, 1923.

SENIOR, N. W.: *Three Lectures on the Value of Money.* Delivered in 1829.

Three Lectures on the Transmission of the Precious Metals. London, 1828.

Three Lectures on the Cost of Obtaining Money. London, 1930. Nos. 3, 4, and 5 in series of reprints of scarce tracts in Economic and Political Science.

SHAH, K. T.: *Trade, Tariffs and Transport in India.* Bombay, 1923.

Sixty Years of Indian Finance. Bombay, 1921.

Indian Currency, Exchange and Banking. Bombay, 1922.

SHIRRAS, G. F.: *Indian Finance and Banking.* London, 1919.

Poverty and Kindred Economic Problems in India. Calcutta, 1932.

"India's Real Balance of Trade in 1922–23." *Proceedings of the Seventh Indian Economic Conference.* 1924.

SMITH, ADAM: *Wealth of Nations.* London, 1776. Cannan Edition, 1922.

SMITH, D. H.: *Economics of Empire Trade.* London, 1930.

SPALDING, W. F.: *Foreign Exchange and Foreign Bills in Theory and in Practice*. London, 1915.

TAUSSIG, F. W.: *International Trade*. New York, 1928.
"Change in Great Britain's Foreign Trade Terms after 1900." *Economic Journal*. 1925.
Selected Readings in International Trade. Boston.
"International Trade under Depreciated Paper." *Quarterly Journal of Economics*. 1917.

THORP, W. S.: *Business Annals*. New York, 1926.

TIWARI, CHANDRIKA PRASAD: *Indian Railways*.

VAKIL, C. N.: *Financial Developments in Modern India*. Bombay, 1924.

VAKIL, C. N., BOSE, S. C., AND DEOLALKAR, P. V.: *Growth of Trade and Industry in Modern India*. Bombay, 1931.

VAKIL, C. N., AND MURANJAN: *Currency and Prices in India*. Bombay, 1926.

VINER, J.: *Canada's Balance of International Indebtedness, 1900–13*. Cambridge, 1924.
Angell's *Theory of International Prices. Journal of Political Economy*. 1926.
"English Theories of Foreign Trade before Adam Smith." *Journal of Political Economy*. 1930.

WATTAL, P. K.: *The System of Financial Administration in British India*. Bombay, 1931.

WHALE, BARRET: *International Trade*. London, 1932.

WHICKSELL, K.: "International Freights and Prices." *Quarterly Journal of Economics*. 1918.

WHITAKER, A. C.: "The Ricardian Theory of Gold Movements and Professor Laughlin's Views on Money." *Quarterly Journal of Economics*. 1904.

WHITTLESEY, C. R.: "Foreign Investment and the Terms of Trade." *Quarterly Journal of Economics*. 1932.

WILLCOX, W. F.: *International Migration*. 2 volumes. The International Bureau of Economic Research, edited by Walter F. Willcox.

WILLIAMS, J. H.: "Latin American Foreign Exchange and International Balances during the War." *Quarterly Journal of Economics*. 1919.

Argentine International Trade under Inconvertible Paper Money, 1880–1900. Cambridge, 1920.

"The Theory of International Trade Reconsidered." *Economic Journal*. 1929.

WILLIAMS, T. T.: "The Rise of Prices in India." *Economic Journal*. 1915.

"India's Present Monetary Condition." *Economic Journal*. 1907. An Anonymous Article.

WILSON, R.: *Capital Imports and the Terms of Trade Examined in the Light of Sixty Years of Australian Borrowings*. Melbourne, 1931.

WOOD, G.: *Borrowing and Business in Australia*. London, 1930.

ZAPOLEON, L. B.: "International and Domestic Commodities and the Theory of Prices." *Quarterly Journal of Economics*. 1931

REPORTS

Census of India, 1891, 1901, 1911, and 1921.

Controller of Currency in India—Annual Reports.

Indian Currency Committees—
- Hershell Committee, 1893.
- Fowler Committee, 1898.
- Chamberlain Commission, 1914.
- Babington-Smith Committee, 1919.
- Hilton-Young Commission, 1924.

Enquiry into the Rise of Prices in India, 5 volumes, 1914.

Indian External Capital Committee, 1925.

Indian Central Banking Enquiry Committee. 2 volumes, 1931.

Indian Post and Telegraphs Department. Annual Reports.

League of Nations: Economic Section—

Balance of payments; Foreign Trade Balances, International Memorandum, 1910–24.

Brussels International Financial Conference, Paper on International Trade.

Memorandum on Credit, Currency and Exchange Fluctuations, by A. C. Pigou.

Memorandum on the Development of the Sea-borne Trade in selected articles in ten years ending 1912–13. Supplement to the *Indian Trade Journal* dated August 14, 1913.

Moral and Material Progress Reports, 1893 to 1914.

Review of the Trade of India, Annual Reports.

STATISTICAL PUBLICATIONS

Index Numbers of India Prices. 2 volumes. Department of Commercial Intelligence and Statistics, 1928.

Prices and Wages in India, Annual Publications.

Sea-borne Trade of British India, Annual Publication.

Statistical Abstracts Relating to British India, 1893 to 1914.

Statistical Abstracts for the United Kingdom, 1893 to 1914.

Statistics of British India, volume iii, Financial Statistics.

INDEX